Someone Once Said

Someone Once Said

*The Preaching Ministry
of Frank Pollard*

Insight Press
2008

Insight Press, Inc.
P.O. Box 5077
Covington, Louisiana 70434

Pollard, Frank, 1934-
Someone once said : the preaching ministry of Frank Pollard / Frank Pollard.
    p. cm.
ISBN 978-0-914520-48-1 (alk. paper)
1. Baptists--Sermons. 2. Sermons, American--20th century. I. Title.
BX6333.P67S66 2008
252'.061--dc22
    2008008690

Thanks to Patricia Ethridge for her work retyping the material for publication.

Cover design by AlphaGraphics.

ISBN: 978-0-9145-204-8-1

Contents

Foreword

One of the great joys of my life has been to follow Frank Pollard as pastor of First Baptist Church Jackson, Mississippi. Dr. Pollard has been a great source of love and encouragement. In addition, he has provided a tremendous example of a pastor who faithfully preaches the Word of God.

Dr. Pollard has faithfully preached the gospel of Jesus Christ for more than four decades. At luncheon I was attending, a man sat across the table from me and told how he had come to know the Lord while kneeling in his living room and praying to the Lord following one of Dr. Pollard's sermons. This man's story mirrors that of countless men and women and boys and girls who have entered into a relationship with God through the faithful preaching of Frank Pollard.

For decades, Dr. Pollard has used his extraordinary gifts of teaching and preaching to reach thousands who have packed the pews to hear his sermons. However, his preaching has not stopped at the church door.

For many years his sermons were heard on the Baptist Hour Radio program on 349 stations around the country. These sermons were played over 1,000 times every week. In addition, 400,000 actual viewers watched his sermons weekly on the ACTS Network and Family Net. Also, for a number of years, his sermons were broadcast on Russian television to a potential viewing audience of 100,000,000.

One of Dr. Pollard's countless honors was being selected in 1979 by Time magazine as one the seven most outstanding Protestant preachers in America. In typical Frank Pollard style, he has always been quick to note that is the same year Time magazine chose the Ayatollah Khomeini as its Man of the Year.

More than a great preacher, however, Dr. Pollard is a great man of God. His humility and gracious spirit are widely known and widely admired. For many years, he has lived out the messages he has preached.

Millions of people have had access to the preaching ministry of Dr. Pollard. Now, through the publication of this book of Frank Pollard sermons, many more will be blessed by his proclamation of the Word of God. May your life be richly blessed, your faith strengthened, and your walk with the Lord enhanced as you experience the preaching ministry of Dr. Frank Pollard.

Stan Buckley
Senior Pastor
First Baptist Church
Jackson, Mississippi

Chapter 1

Growth in Priorities

Matthew 6:24–34

I never saw an absent-minded professor—not in four years of college and four more years of graduate study. Unfortunately, they always remembered everything they told their students to do! You and I have heard many stories concerning absent-minded professors. One such tale pictures the professor at breakfast with his family. His wife said, "Now remember, honey, that today we are moving to the new house. When you come home after work, remember to go to the new house." All day he kept wondering what he was supposed to remember. When the day was over, he went home to the old house. It was empty. There were no people or furnishings. "Now I remember," he said, "I'm supposed to go to the new house." But he couldn't remember where the new house was located. He decided he'd go out in the neighborhood and ask if anyone knew where he could find his new house. There was a little boy playing in the yard. "Young man," he asked, "Do you know where the people who used to live here have moved?" The little boy looked up at him and replied, "Mother said you'd forget."

Now that's absent-minded! But not nearly as tragically absent-minded as the person who breathes God's air, lives only because of God's providence, exists only a heartbeat away from confronting God in judgment, yet forgets Him and lives each day as though God were not.

Wise people learn early that life must have its priorities. Few things really matter, but those that do matter mighty much. Life's largest blunders are caused when people give their first-rate loyalties to third-rate causes.

Here our Lord talks about the greatest priority of all. "No one can be a slave of two masters: He will hate one and love the other; he will be loyal to one and despise the other. You cannot serve both God and money" (Matthew 6:24 GNB).

Every one of us has a master. We are made to be mastered. Those who deny that idea the most illustrate it the best. Some say, "I am a self-made man!" Usually their lives are tragic examples of unskilled labor! Have you noticed how so many who say, "I am the master of my fate; I am the captain of my soul" are servants of liquor or lust or greed?

When Jesus Christ said, "You cannot serve both God and money" He certainly struck an American nerve, didn't He? Countless multitudes worship daily at the altar of riches. How many bow in total admiration before the image engraved on a dollar bill!

Yet we can't live without money, can we? Nor is our Lord asking us to. The things of life are given of God to serve us. The sin comes when we serve the things.

In verses 19 through 21, our Lord lays out some Christian principles of possessing. Listen: "Do not store up riches for yourselves here on earth, where moths and rust destroy, and robbers break in and steal. Instead, store up riches for yourselves in heaven, where moths and rust cannot destroy, and robbers cannot break in and steal. For your heart will always be where your riches are" (Matthew 6:19–21 GNB). In this passage, Jesus teaches us lessons in divine economics.

First, that which can be lost is not really owned. Anything possessed on this earth is subject to the moths of inflation, the rust of depreciation, and the ravages of the thousand-and-one variety of thieves that inhabit this earth. No man is wealthy to whom the grave brings bankruptcy.

Second, eternal investment is wisest. "Store up riches for yourselves in heaven." He is saying, "I know you have a desire to possess, I made you that way. Store up your riches, but put them in a place where you can't lose them. Let them draw interest, compounded to your account throughout eternity." Why is this so important? Because we always look after our investments. "For your heart will always be where your riches are." Instead of letting money be your God, let it lead you closer to God. Invest it in the kingdom of heaven, and it will bring your heart closer to Him. We always look after our investments. Life is lived at its best when we refuse to let the dollar bill be bigger than God. "You cannot serve both God and money." This is a truth that matters mighty much!

It matters much because putting God first in your life is the only way you'll ever be able to overcome life-strangling anxiety. Hear Him speak to you in verses 25 through 34:

This is why I tell you: do not be worried about the food and drink you need in order to stay alive, or about clothes for your body. After all, isn't life worth more than food? And isn't the body worth more than clothes? Look at the birds flying around: They do not plant seeds, gather a harvest and put it in barns; yet your Father in heaven takes care of them! Aren't you worth much more than birds? Can any of you live a bit longer by worrying about it?

And why worry about clothes? Look how the wild flowers grow: They do not work or make clothes for themselves. But I tell you that not even King Solomon with all his wealth had clothes as beautiful as one of these flowers. It is God who clothes the wild grass—grass that is here today and gone tomorrow, burned up in the oven. Won't he be all the more sure to clothe you? What little faith you have!

So do not start worrying: "Where will my food come from? or my drink? or my clothes?" (These are the things the pagans are always concerned about.) Your Father in heaven knows that you need all these things. Instead, be concerned above everything else with the Kingdom of God and with what he requires of you, and he will provide you with all these other things. So do not worry about tomorrow; it will have enough worries of its own. There is no need to add to the troubles each day brings.
(Matthew 6:25–34 GNB).

You who are so anxious about what you'll wear and how you'll eat, look. All around you is evidence that God is well able to take care of what He has created.

"Look at the birds," said Jesus, probably pointing to sparrows. "They are brown, common, song-less, not worth five for two cents in the market, yet the Heavenly Father takes care of them. Aren't you worth much more than birds?"

Some poetic soul penned this delightful ditty:

Said the robin to the sparrow, "I should really like to know
Why these anxious human beings rush about and worry so."
Said the sparrow to the robin, "Friend, I think that must be
That they have no Heavenly Father such as cares for you and me."

Wild lilies grow on the hillside during the rainy season in Israel. "Look at those flowers," said our Lord. "Solomon was never dressed that well. If God can dress up a flower, don't you think He can clothe you?"

Jesus concludes this section of His discourse by telling us that it all depends on our putting God first in our priorities. Verses 33 and 34 promise that when we make Him first He will see to our needs, and we can live life to its fullest one day at a time.

Please know that our Lord is not recommending laziness. The birds He uses as examples still must seek food for themselves and their young. Work is in His will for us. Worry is not. To be active is good; to be anxious is sinful.

Two years ago I visited with Bishop Fulton Sheen. "God has called me to preach," I said. "Talk to me about how to preach." I'll never forget the look in those piercing eyes as he replied, "No, I won't talk to you about how to preach. Preaching is a gift of God. It's like being a good businessman or a pretty girl. God gave you the gift but you are responsible for developing it and using it."

That's true of your life. Whatever gift you have, God gave it to you. You are responsible to Him for what you do with it. Some of you have not discovered your gift because you've not given your life to Him. You may be all tied up, anxious about making a living. If so, please hear Him say, "Friend, I'm not only concerned about your having a living, I want you to have a life." "But seek ye first the kingdom of God, and His righteousness; and all these things shall be added unto you."

Chapter 2

What Does God Expect of Us?

Luke 16:1–13

I had traveled all the way to New York City to talk to him about preaching. Sitting in his living room, I was thrilled to be visiting with one of the most effective media ministers of all time. When television was young, he appeared on prime-time television on Sunday evenings, teaching the Bible. He was fully sponsored by Admiral Corporation. His broadcasts appeared opposite Frank Sinatra and Milton Berle, the biggest stars of his day. His audience was fifteen to twenty million viewers. In 1952 the Academy of Television Arts and Sciences named Fulton Sheen the most outstanding personality on television. When accepting the award he said, "I want to thank my writers: Matthew, Mark, Luke and John."

During the visit, he looked at me with those famous penetrating eyes and said, "You have come to New York City to talk to me about preaching? I do not know what to say. Preaching is a gift. It is like being a beautiful woman. She is not responsible for having her beauty, but she is very responsible for what she does with it."

Everything we have is a gift from God. Our time, our talents, our resources are all gifts from God. Like beauty and brilliance, we are not responsible for having them, but we are very responsible for what we do with them. Our salvation, our lives are gifts of God's grace. The Bible teaches that Christians can manage these gifts in a manner that will result in our attaining unlimited, unfading, guaranteed riches.

This is the theme of one of our Lord's most puzzling parables. Our Lord told His disciples (it is not a story for people who are not Christians) about a rich man who had a slave acting as a steward, like Joseph's role in Potiphar's house in the Genesis 39 story. The steward was responsible for managing his master's vast holdings. Someone suggested to the rich man that his steward was mishandling the money, squandering it, spending the money indiscriminately.

The steward was called on the carpet and told to settle his affairs and get the books in order and get out.

In wide-eyed panic, this dishonest manager began to ponder his future. "What in the world will I do? I am too lazy to work. I am too proud to beg. What will I do?" The wheels in his brain began to turn counter-clockwise. His brain wheels were conditioned to turn in the wrong direction. His mind, greased by greed and expediency, worked rapidly. "I have it," he thought, "I will call in my master's debtors and reduce their debts, falsifying their accounts. Then, because I have helped them, they will be obligated to help me. If they do not feel obligated enough, I will have material for blackmail because they will have a part in the crime."

He called the debtors in one by one. "How much do you owe?" "One hundred measures of oil." "Then change it to fifty," said the steward. Another debtor came to his desk. "What is your debt?" "One hundred measures of wheat," he answered. "Then take the pen and write down eighty." And so it went. When the master discovered this trickery he was—well, he was impressed. Surely he was disturbed, certainly he was angry, and the steward did lose his job. But the master was also impressed. Jesus, the author of this story, says there is something in the bad man's action that is a good example. He said, "This fellow is a shrewd dude. He is a crook but he is clever in a way you need to emulate."

What is the lesson of this puzzling parable? It is this: Life as he had experienced it would soon be over. His days as a free-wheeling spender of another man's wealth were ending. He took steps to prepare for living beyond that abrupt ending.

In this story, our Lord teaches us lessons in life management. Here is His emphasis: No matter how much or how little you may have in ability, opportunity, or wealth, you can manage your life in such a way as to be really rich.

If you would be truly successful, you must know and live by the laws of life management; then you will reap the rewards of life management. What we have, we have by the grace of God. The principles of life management are built on the solid foundation of the grace of almighty God.

In the first chapter of Ephesians, this foundation is spelled out with remarkable clarity. The Word declares that we have been selected by the Father because He loves us. We have been saved by the Son who died on the cross because of that love. We have been sealed by the Holy Spirit, assured of our salvation forever because of the love of our wonderful God and His grace. Life management is not about getting into heaven. All who come to Christ will be in heaven. This is about reward in heaven. There is nothing you can do to save your soul except turn to God in repentance and faith in Jesus Christ.

Life management is a principle only for Christians. It has to do with living life in such a way as to one day hear Him say, "Well done, good and faithful servant. Because you have been faithful in a very little thing, you will be in authority over very much." Successful living demands that you know and keep the laws of life management.

Here are three laws of life management.

Law Number One: Do your best with what you have. It does not matter in God's eyes how much you have but how well you handle it. Barnabas was praised for his large gift of land to the early church. The widow was lauded by our Lord for her gift of less than a penny. Someone said, "I am but one, but I am one. I cannot do much but I can do something. What I can do, I ought to do. What I ought to do, by the grace of God, I will do."

The Bible commands, "Whatsoever ye do, do it all to the glory of God," (1 Corinthians 10:31).

I heard a preacher tell about a shoe cobbler who was buried a Scottish cemetery. His tombstone declared that for fifty years he had cobbled shoes to the glory of God.

Luke 16:10 (NAS) says, "He who is faithful in a very little thing is faithful also in much." Eugene Peterson's translation declares, "If you're honest in small things, you'll be honest in big things. . . . . If you're not honest in small jobs, who will put you in charge of the store?" The first law of life management: Do your best with what you have.

Law Number Two: What we manage is not ours. A while back I read of a strange thief in Hamburg, Germany. There was not a single brick, tile, screw, or nail in his neat little house that had not been stolen. Over a period of two years and by way of eighty different thefts, he acquired every square inch of his house at someone else's expense. He even admitted he had stolen the flowers blooming in his front yard. Day by day, bit by bit, he accomplished his theft. His actions parallel the spiritually crippled behavior of many men and women. Day by day they appropriate the things of God, His air, His sunshine, His food. They take everything He gives and uses them for selfish purposes. Actually they embezzle a life because they give nothing in return. In building their life every single brick, tile, screw, and nail is stolen.

All of us are like the steward, handling for a while the property of another. "The earth is the LORD's," declares the Bible, "and everything in it," (Psalm 24:1). If it is true that that which can be lost is not really owned—and it is true—then not even our lives are ours. The steward was a slave. He belonged to his master. "In him we live and move and have our being" (Acts 17:28 KJV). Life, breath, and all things come from Him.

Our time, our talents and our resources are all His, given by His grace, controlled by His providence. If we are Christians, we have accepted the fact that He is our loving Master and we will give an accounting to Him.

How sad to see people steal a life from the Master and then realize they are stuck with what they stole. Have you heard Edwin Markham's tale of a wealthy man who assigned a contractor friend to build a beautiful home? When the plans and specifications were agreed upon, the rich man left on an extended trip. The builder, with no one around to check on him, proceeded to cheat on every specification of the house. Floors, beams, walls, and roof were of the cheapest material, all built on a flimsy and poor foundation. When the rich man returned, he sought out the builder and said, "Keep the keys; they are the keys to your house. You did not know it, but you were building this house for yourself." A constant warning from God's Word is this: People who embezzle their lives from God are stuck with what they stole.

Life management is to do your best with what you have. It is to know that what we manage is not ours.

Law No. 3: The things we manage are not real. In Luke 16:11

is a heavy question, "If you have not been trustworthy in handling worldly wealth, who will trust you with true riches?" "True riches" means authentic, genuine, permanent wealth. The wealth of this world is not real because it does not last.

The goods we now manage are temporary. Life's largest blunder is to act as though this were not so. "Their inward thought," said the psalmist, "is, that their houses shall continue for ever, and their dwelling places to all generations; they call their lands after their own names," (Psalm 49:11). This is sheer mockery. "For," as the Bible says of one who lusts after the treasures of earth, "when he dieth he shall carry nothing away." (v. 17 KJV).

Alexander the Great was born to one empire and conquered another. He possessed the wealth of both the East and the West, yet he commanded that when carried to his grave, his hands should be left unwrapped and outside the funeral bier so that all might see them empty.

The great Charlemagne was, at his request, buried sitting on his throne, wearing his crown, robe, and jewels. In his lap was an open Bible and his dead finger was resting on Mark 8:36, "for what shall it profit a man, if he shall gain the whole world, and lose his own soul?"

Successful life management is a matter of exchanging a life you cannot keep for a life you cannot lose. It is trading the temporary goods of this world for unending, secure treasure.

No matter how much or how little you may have in ability, opportunity, or wealth, you can manage your life in such a way as to be really rich.

Chapter 3

Forgive Yourself

Matthew 18:21–35

We hear the word *center* a lot. First, it was the shopping center. Now there are sewing centers, food centers, and entertainment centers. Some churches, disdaining the stuffy connotations of the word *sanctuary* call the place where people worship the worship center.

I think churches ought to be known as forgiveness centers. The New Testament describes the church as a family of the loved and the loving, the forgiven and the forgiving. It is in Christ that you find forgiveness. It is in Christ that you become a forgiving person.

Jesus never said, "I am come that you might have guilt and have it more abundantly." He said, "I have come that they may have life, and have it to the full" (John 10:10).

You may think the church is more a guilt center than a forgiveness center. Many professing Christians are preoccupied with guilt. We carry it around all the time. Our guilt robs us of so much! It also robs others of what we could give them. The one thing that keeps most of us from our Father's business is preoccupation with our own guilt.

Guilt is not something that will vanish if you simply deny it. You may sear your conscience, but it's like varnishing rotten wood or painting over rust. You may cover it up for a while, but the problem is still there.

In a moment of reality, a wise friend may counsel, "You must forgive yourself. You must accept yourself."

You reply, "You're right. I know it, but how do I do it?"

The friend says, "You must do it."

You say, "How?"

And the wise friend is silent, but the Word of God is vocal!

To this vital issue, four questions are posed: (1) Have you accepted Jesus Christ as Savior and Lord? (2) Are you majoring on your guilt or His grace? (3) Can you forgive others? (4) Can you forgive yourself?

Inscribe this indelibly in your mind and heart—you cannot be free of your guilt unless Jesus Christ is your Lord. I am not asking you to try to begin living a Christian life. You can't do it. I'm asking you to confess your sinfulness to God, admit your total lack of power to save yourself, and receive by faith the forgiveness that comes only through Jesus Christ. He said, "I am the way and the truth and the life. No one comes to the Father except through me" (John 14:6).

A non-Christian is separated from God by true moral guilt. If you are not a Christian, you feel guilty because you *are* guilty. The Bible declares that we are all sinners, both by mistake and by intention. This true guilt is removed only by the Christ who took our sins upon Himself on the cross and became the sacrificial Lamb of God.

Our guilt is removed only on the basis of the finished work of Christ plus nothing on our part. There must be no humanistic note added at any point in our accepting the gospel. Ephesians 2:8–9 declares, "For it is by grace you have been saved [an accomplished fact], through faith. . . . It is the gift of God—not by works, so that no one can boast."

When we believe God and accept Christ's sacrifice on the cross as full payment for our sins, the Bible asserts we are justified by God. The guilt is gone! The instrument for receiving this forgiveness is faith. This is not faith in faith. It is not a leap in the dark. It is faith in the specific promises of God.

When you no longer turn your back on God, when you no longer call God a liar, when you lift up empty hands of faith and accept the finished work of Christ on the cross, you are passed from death into life. This is what it means to be born again. This is the first and most indispensable step in learning to forgive yourself. You can never *feel* forgiven until you *are* forgiven.

The next question is: Are you majoring on your guilt or His grace? Do you think more of how bad you are or how good He is? In the mid-1950s, some seminary students noticed that many of the people who spoke in chapel were converted gangsters, murderers, drug addicts, and others whose lifestyle had not been recommended in the Sunday school quarterly. Each spelled out in sensational detail his sorry past and ended by telling how he had become a Christian.

One morning, there appeared on a prominent campus bulletin board a giant poster with the heading: "How to Be a Great Evangelist!" Listed were statements like: "Be an ex-convict. Be an ex-murderer. Be an ex-drug addict." At the end of the last statement was an asterisk guiding you to some tiny print at the bottom, which read, "If you have none of these requirements, we suggest you take two years off and establish your background."

This was not to discredit the work of God's grace in those lives but to point out that the biblical emphasis is upon His grace and not in the detailing of our sins. Christians are to exalt Christ, not parade our past sins.

We never read in Holy Writ of David saying, "I committed murder and adultery. Now my whole household is in rebellion. My own sons are fighting me. One of my sons raped my daughter. You should have seen me in the good old days when I was God's man." We don't read that in Scripture. We read of David saying, "I have sinned against the Lord," and Nathan replying, "And the Lord has put away your sin." Then David resumes his life as God's man.

Can you imagine a first-century gathering? The pastor gets up and says, "Have we got an exciting testimony for you tonight! I want you to meet Brother Paul. He'll tell you what an awful man he's been!" Then Paul gets up and rehashes it again. He tells them how bad he's been—how he murdered Christians and plundered the church, and how many people were misled by his intellect, his teaching, and his denial of Jesus Christ. Why, he would be sensational! What crowds would gather!

While that story is in Acts as a part of the church's history, it was not the main topic of Paul's message. It was not his preoccupation. He didn't waste his time or others' by posing as the hero of his own sins. Rather, he exalted Christ as the hero of his forgiveness.

The main thrust of his message was, "Therefore, if anyone is in Christ, he is a new creation; the old has gone [no matter how bad or horrible or how many people were involved], the new has come!" (2 Corinthians 5:17).

Paul exalted Christ rather than wallowing in the garbage of

his life; that garbage had already been dumped in the sea of God's forgetfulness. On almost every page of the Holy Writ, Christians are commanded to dwell in the high places of praise and gratitude to Him for His grace. What a shame that so many unnecessarily wallow in the garbage dump of their past sins!

Listen anew to Paul say, "Forgetting what is behind and straining toward what is ahead, I press on toward the goal to win the prize for which God has called me heavenward in Christ Jesus" (Philippians 3:13–14).

A secret of the forgiving heart is this: If you'll stop magnifying your guilt, you'll stop magnifying the guilt of others. If you "turn your eyes upon Jesus," think about His forgiving grace and praise Him for it, then you become more like Him. That forgiving grace not only works in you but also through you.

Thus, the next question is: Can you forgive others? In the sixth chapter of Matthew, Christ teaches us a model prayer. One line declares, "Forgive us our debts, as we also have forgiven our debtors" (Matthew 6:12). This is the only part of the prayer that Jesus chose to explain in greater detail. Immediately after the "Amen" He said, "For if you forgive men when they sin against you, your heavenly Father will also forgive you. But if you do not forgive men their sins, your Father will not forgive your sins" (Matthew 6:14–15).

In many different ways, our Lord lays this heavy truth upon us. In Matthew 18:21–35, we find Simon Peter asking Jesus, in essence, "How much do we have to take? How many times do we have to forgive someone? Is seven times enough?"

Jesus answered, "Not just seven times, but seventy times seven."

Now I don't think our Lord meant—do you?—that on the four-hundred-ninety-first time, Peter could clobber someone instead of forgiving them. He was asking, "How many times has God forgiven you?"

Then he told a story of a man who owed someone a greater fortune than Palestine's national budget. It was a debt so staggering he could never hope to repay it. When payment was due, he begged for mercy and, amazingly, received it! In one minute, he was under the burden of an unimaginable debt. The next, he was forgiven the debt. By an unbelievable grace, the debt was stamped "paid in full," though he had not paid one penny.

After this experience, the forgiven man confronted someone who owed him twenty dollars. He rejected his debtor's pleas for mercy and had him thrown in jail. When the word of this got around, his benefactor called the man in and said, "You are wicked! How could you receive multiplied millions of dollars worth of forgiveness and not forgive a twenty-dollar debt?"

The application is readily apparent. All of us who know Jesus deserve hell, yet we have been given heaven. Our sins deserve punishment, yet we've been given free pardon. How can we, who know God's great love, not forgive? When He has said to all who have sinned, "Neither do I condemn thee," how can we condemn others? When we know the truth that "There is now no condemnation for those who are in Christ Jesus" (Romans 8:1), how can we condemn others?

You may say, "Wait a minute, preacher. This sermon is entitled 'Forgive Yourself.' You've talked about God forgiving us and our forgiving others, but you've not yet addressed the main topic." Friend, these four questions are progressive. You must answer "yes" to each one in order before you can answer the next.

The first, indispensable question is: Is Christ your Savior? Have you come to Him, confessing your sinfulness, asking His forgiveness, knowing His death on the cross is full and complete payment for your sin? Guilt will gnaw on you in life and consume you in eternity unless you receive Him as your Savior.

Secondly, if you are forgiven, are you living like a forgiven person? Do you praise Him and make Him the hero of your forgiveness? No matter what you have done, no matter how much water has gone over the dam, He owns the dam and the water. Praise Him for His love and grace.

If you have been forgiven and you live like a forgiven person, then you will be a forgiving person. When you are a forgiving person, then you can even forgive yourself. When this happens, you have learned and can joyfully share the liberating experience of being saved by the grace of God!

Chapter 4

Making the Most of the Rest of Your Life

2 Timothy 4:6–8

Life is a paper white
on which each one of us may write
his word or two and then comes night.

If life is a sentence with a capital letter beginning at our birth and a period at our death, then there are all sorts of punctuation marks in between. Every now and then, put a comma in your life. Slow down a minute and ask some basic questions, such as, "How am I doing?" Maybe ask, "How do I make the most of the rest of my life?" Ask yourself if it's possible to get up each day with an inner confidence and say, "I am living, and living well!" When the day comes that you won't be able to get up, you can look up and see nothing but rewards and joy and say, "The best is yet to be." Is that possible?

There lived a man who had no illusions about his imperfections. "I am the chief of all sinners," he wrote in this his last letter. He had made no discernible impact on his world. He had started a few struggling churches in the population centers of his day and these churches brought him both joy and heartache. There were no buildings that bore his name. He accumulated no wealth. He had no family. He spent many of his most productive years as a political prisoner because religion had been reduced to a political power game in his day. Yet he could write these words reflecting on his life and on the eternity ahead, "For I am already being poured out like a drink offering, and the time has come for my departure. I have fought the good fight, I have finished the race, I have kept the faith. Now there is in store for me the crown of righteousness, which the Lord, the righteous Judge, will award to me on that day—and not only to me, but also to all who have longed for His appearing," (2 Timothy 4:6–8).

It sounds almost like bragging, doesn't it? "I have fought the good fight, I have finished the race, I have kept the faith, I am going to get the crown." These lines were born not in proud egotism but in loving encouragement. You see, he was writing to his younger friend, Timothy, saying, "Since I have met our Lord, I have made the most of my life. Now I encourage you to make the most of the rest of your life." He was simply telling how he lived, so Timothy could know how to live well. God in His love and wisdom made these words His words, and through them He is telling you and me how to make the most of the rest of our lives.

It is, of course, a choice. The fire that burns in the hearts of those that make the most of life is not started by spontaneous combustion. It is no accident. If the fire burns in you, that fire must be set deliberately. You say, "I will give myself to a purpose worth hurting for." "I have fought the good fight," Paul said. The Greek word for fought is *agon*. We get our word *agony* from it. Life lived all the way up is a life lived for a purpose worth hurting for.

The Olympic games have as their motto, "Peace, Joy, and Love." Those who compete in those events all say that they achieve their goals by learning to live with PAT in their training and their discipline. P stands for pain, A for agony, and T for torture. They know that in order to reach their goal of Olympic glory, to share the peace and love of Olympic glory with others who compete, they must train through the pain, agony, and torture. Hear Paul's testimony of assurance; that fighting the good fight is worth it. Making the most of life means giving your life to a cause worth hurting for. In 2 Corinthians 4:8, Paul says, "We are hard pressed on every side, but not crushed; perplexed, but not in despair; persecuted, but not abandoned; struck down, but not destroyed. We always carry around in our body the death of Jesus, so that the life of Jesus may also be revealed in our body." While he lived, he was reckoned to be a man of little consequence, yet he would be known as one of the world's greatest personalities. The small, struggling, bickering, sinning churches he started would become seeds of a worldwide harvest. From the days of his imprisonment would come letters that would become part of the eternal Word of God. He didn't measure his life by what he could produce, but by what he could give to it.

His impact, which seemed so small and weak to him, would become great. He had no way of knowing that. His only desire was simply to do what was open to him to do.

Parents, you are committed to rearing your children in the ways of God. There is an agony and pain in that task, but who knows what God will do with the child of your responsibility?

Sunday School teachers who give themselves to the task may see little in it. There is some agony and pain in preparation and dedication to being in your place, mentally, physically, and spiritually on the Lord's Day. If you fight the good fight, who knows how God will use your effort?

I went to my hometown to thank a godly, successful businessman for being my Sunday school teacher and a great example in my life and he said, "I never thought you were even listening."

You who witness to your faith know that there is some pain in that, the agony of rejection and the sacrifice of time to share your faith. You can know you are doing the thing God calls His people to do, and you measure your success not by what you have accomplished, but by what you have given to it. Making the most of the rest of your life means giving yourself to a cause worth hurting for.

"I have fought the good fight." It means being committed to going the distance.

"I have finished the race." I have committed to run to the end.

Some have said it was the greatest speech in the history of western civilization. Winston Churchill was eighty-one years of age. He was asked to speak about his judgment on the most important factor in changing history. What is the most vital thing for people to do? Reporters, the king and queen, and all of Parliament were there. After a tremendous ovation, the bulldog of Great Britain, his lower jaw jutting forth, put his left hand on top of his cane and his right hand on top of that, leaned forward and gave his greatest speech. It was seven words long. He said, "Never give up." Then eyeing everyone in the whole audience, this great lion of Manchester said, "Never, never give up."

If you would make the most of the rest of your life, you must have a cause worth hurting for, you must be committed to going the distance, and you must be a good manager of what has been entrusted to you.

"I have kept the faith." In the athletic picture Paul is using he says, "I have played by the rules." To King Agrippa in the Book of Acts, he said, "I have not been disobedient to my heavenly calling." To the Thessalonians he wrote, "I am thankful to have been entrusted with the gospel." He had not forgotten, abused, neglected or misused this wonderful thing that had been placed in his care. He had continually told the story of Jesus Christ.

All of these statements, "I have fought the good fight, I have finished the race, I have kept the faith," are stated in the perfect tense, meaning something is completed with results that abide. The fight and the race are over, but the resulting victory is forever. "I have spent my days in getting up each morning with a cause worth hurting for and a commitment to finish the race, and because I have done that," he says, "as I enter the time when I can no longer get up, I can look up and see nothing but joy and reward. Now there is in store for me the crown of righteousness."

In verse 6 he declares that the last drops of his life offering to God are dripping out. The time has come for his departure. *Departure* is a traveling term. It is a ship leaving one destination and heading for another. One translation of this verse says, "The time has come for me to sail away." He is facing death with a confidence that he is departing for a far better destination.

Leisel Goodman said, "The more complete one's life is, the less one fears death." People are not afraid of death, per se, but the incompleteness of their lives. We all know you'll make the most of the rest of your life when you realize that far more than most of the rest of your life will be spent in eternity.

You may say, "Preacher, you're talking about me. There is no way I can be that ready and that confident. I haven't accomplished too much for our Lord." Paul didn't think he had, either. I heard Billy Graham say on national television this week that he thought his life had been a failure.

When I see the things happening in our city and in our state and reflect that for almost twenty-five years of my life I have tried to lead this church to have an impact on our city and state, I, too, feel a deep despair and failure. Paul could not look back from that damp prison cell and see accomplishments. His confidence was in the fact that he did what he could.

You may say, "But I have not done what I could; I have lived selfishly and sinfully." Well, much of Paul's life had not been lived in the will of God. He thought he was doing the right thing but he came to realize that what he had thought to be so valuable and worthwhile in his life was literally waste and garbage, and he turned from that. You can make the most of the rest of your life by turning from that which is not pleasing to God.

You may say, "But I'm a sinner." We can all say that; those who don't are lying. See 1 John 1:8. Paul called himself in this last letter the chief of all sinners.

How then did he earn his crown of righteousness? He didn't earn it. He said, "It will be given to me." The Lord, who alone is righteous, gives us right standing with God. How do we make the most of the rest of our lives? We begin today by saying, "I give myself, Lord, to You. Even if it means agony, I give myself to You knowing that loving and serving You is worth hurting for. I will not quit. I will not give up. I will keep running the race until the time of my departure or until Jesus comes. I thank you for entrusting me with the gospel. I pray that you will help me live so that others will see Christ in me."

As you give yourself to Him, know Him, love Him, and serve Him, then you begin to look forward to His return. One day, Gabriel will plant one foot on earth and the other in heaven and sound a clear note on his trumpet, and every person on earth will hear and they will know the King is coming. The King is coming, and that will not frighten or alarm you because the King is your Lord and Master, and also your friend, whom you know by His first name. Today is the first day of the rest of your life.

Today, decide for Jesus. In Him, you find a cause worth hurting for. In Him, you find a race worth finishing. In Him, you find a faith worth keeping. In Him, you have victory in life and over sin and even over time, for when you link your life to Him, you are never really going to die. Make the most of the rest of your life. Give it to Jesus.

Chapter 5

It's Time to Pray

Joel 2:12-17

Our president has called this nation to prayer. He has asked that we set aside this coming Thursday as a day of national prayer.

Joel called the people of his day to prayer. He said, "Blow the trumpet." It's time to pray.

In chapter 1 and the beginning of chapter 2, Joel describes an invasion of locusts upon the land. In the Old Testament, a plague of locusts was a much-used picture of great trouble. Nothing but annihilating war was worse than a locust invasion.

Flying locusts would come in such great numbers they would blacken the sky and blot out the light of the sun. Crawling locusts would come, line after line, like an invading army, conquering every inch of the land, devouring any green and growing thing and leaving nothing behind but larvae to hatch more locusts.

How splendid an image, then, for the prophet to use in describing the crisis of God's people. Moral corruption had become the accepted way of life. The locusts had come.

Centuries later, God would inspire John to recall the words of our Lord Christ, "This is the verdict: Light has come into the world, but men loved darkness instead of light because their deeds were evil." The locusts had come and had darkened the sky. The people were still religious. They were making the meetings, doing the ceremony, but it was mostly surface. They talked *about* God but not *to* Him. They sang the praise songs, said the praise words, but without praise in their hearts. The judgment caused by their own sinful deeds was just around the corner and they didn't know. The world around them watched and because of them, God's name was a joke, their connection to Him a subject of scorn.

Joel's word was, "Wake up! Wake up! It's time to pray!"

There are more cracks in our sinful culture than in any other nation before us.

Racism is our greatest blight. In nations of old and present, we are appalled that they put newborn babies in the streets to die. We kill them in the womb before we have to look at them. Wake up! Wake up! It's time to pray!

Citizens of our city lock themselves in their own homes, afraid to venture out, especially at night, for fear of their lives. Trust in our government is eroding with the coming of each day's news. Wake up! Wake up! It's time to pray!

Some of our best young athletes say they can't stand the pressure of being rich and famous, so they turn to drugs. Others, some of them our best young people, say they can't stand the pressure of being poor and unknown and they too turn to drugs and alcohol for release, destroying themselves and doing irreparable hurt to all who love them. Wake up! Wake up! It's time to pray!

Judgment has come upon the nation and we are too blind to see it. Wake up! Wake up! It's time to pray!

The name of our Lord has become a national laughingstock. Every day all our senses are bombarded with reports of the alleged misdoings of a few ministers. (Thank God that's still rare enough to be news.) While joking about the foolish activity of media ministers who have tried to marry the ways of this world to the work of God, comedians, commentators, cartoonists, and columnists are blaspheming the precious name of our Lord God. Wake up! Wake up! It's time to pray!

I fear many people come to church but never see God. They sing songs with words they neither hear or believe. A lost and dying world around us sees little sign that God's people really care. The sinful, earthy, lustful lifestyles of people of the church give little evidence of the presence of God in them. Wake up! Wake up! It's time to pray!

Any right approach to our Lord will balance celebration and conviction. One of our sharp, bright-eyed young people was telling why she likes First Baptist Church. "In some churches, it is 'Low in the grave He lay,' but here it is 'Up from the grave He arose!' " We must never lose that sense of happy celebration. But the spiritual balance must be there too, the holy hush of deep conviction.

During Golden Gate Seminary's inaugural ceremonies last week, there were many speakers. Most were there to bring greetings from sister Southern Baptist agencies and institutions. They were mercifully short and clever in their remarks. Each short and clever statement was followed by the applause of an appreciative audience. But when the man being officially installed as president of the seminary spoke, it was different and the reason was different. He spoke from a deep conviction, a loving heart and with great hope in God for the present and future. When he finished his statements, there was no applause, only a holy hush, for God had spoken in a different way.

This is a parable for God's people. Sometimes people applaud out of a sense of thanks to God. Sometimes a congregation sees itself only as an audience and applauds what is perceived to be an artful and clever performance. But there should be times when God speaks in song or testimony or lesson or sermon and we don't applaud; we repent, we rededicate, we worship and adore Him.

Along with our moments of holy celebration must come the convicting times when the only proper response is a holy hush.

Verse 12 declares that now is the time to pray. "Even now" declares the Lord, "return to me with your heart." Do it now! He commands, while there is time.

All of my years as a minister of the gospel, I have sought out older ministers, to learn from them. It used to be a lot easier to find older ministers than it is now. Consistently I have asked them one question, "If you could do it again, what would you change?" For all these years the answers I received have been virtually unanimous: "I would pray more."

Lest you think this is limited to the experience of religious professionals, I can tell you of no fewer than twenty friends, active, busy people who begin their day in quiet time with God. God's Word to us is: Blow the trumpet. Don't wait.

God calls all of us to prayer, the whole assembly, all the people. You children are called to prayer, even the babies. You who are elders are called to prayer. Your prayers mean so much. You, who are newly wed, busy, enraptured with each other and your new life, God calls you to prayer.

Let all of us minister before the Lord. It is amazing how hard it is for ministers to really pray. But we must wake up! It's time for all of us to pray!

"'Even now,' declares the Lord, 'return to me with all your heart, with fasting and weeping and mourning. Rend your hearts and not your garments.'" They had a tradition of tearing their clothing as a show of repentance and godly sorrow. God is declaring: "I don't want the show of repentance; I want the reality."

In the last part of verse 17, He says to pray like this, "Spare your people, O LORD. Don't let others make fun of you because of the actions of your people. Don't let your Holy name become a by-word as people look at us and say I wonder what has become of their God?" It's time to pray, "Our Father, which art in heaven, hallowed by Thy name."

Look at verse 13. "Return to the LORD your God, for He is gracious and compassionate, slow to anger and abounding in love, and He relents from sending calamity." That is, He likes to change his mind about punishing us.

God is a loving gracious Father and He begs us to put ourselves in a position of blessing.

Many parents know what it is to love a child, to want to bless that child with every good thing possible. But acts of the child prohibit it.

See that young couple, wanting, praying for a child? Finally it happens. The child is born. What thanks to God are given! What a joy, what a delight. In those early years, everything is done to ensure that the child will grow and develop physically, socially, emotionally, and spiritually.

But in teen years, the pressure of peers and the influence of a society that has lost its values begins to take its toll. Disturbing, telltale signs are at first ignored, dismissed as the normal confusions of adolescent growth. But soon those signs of alcohol or drug abuse cannot be ignored. There are times of advice, lectures, threats, fights, and counselors. But to no avail. The ugly thing has the most precious thing in your life in a death grip, it seems. For this child does not want to change, will not change. And the destructive, self-imposed judgment continues. And the parents who would gladly sacrifice every worldly possession and literally give their lives for that child can do nothing.

Our Heavenly Father is in that same position. Our sins have blocked His blessings. This Lord, who is gracious and compassionate and slow to anger and abounding in love, knows that sinful people would take any of His gracious gifts and use them wrongly, to their further destruction, so He can do nothing. So the destruction, the self-imposed judgment comes. But if we return to Him with all our hearts, we have changed that. We are now in the position of blessing.

Wake up! Wake up! It's time to pray!

Chapter 6

Love of Power / Power of Love

Matthew 2

The Christmas story is full of contrasts and extremes. There are royalty and stables. There are gold and rich gifts and poverty. There's the purest person ever born in the filthiest place imaginable. The starkest contrast of all is between King Herod and Jesus Christ.

Herod is the epitome of what is wrong in your heart and mine. He is the clearest expression of the sin in each of us. Christ is pure. The baby born in Bethlehem would never sin. He would become everything God had in mind when He said, "Now I'll make a man!" He is the highest expression of all that is good. King Herod was the finished product of the love of power. Jesus Christ is the perfect example and the only source of the power of love. The potential for both is offered to you and me. Christmas calls us to face that.

King Herod, like many today, believed life is measured by power. The original sin in Eden was in answer to the question, "Who's in charge?" This sin affects how we do business and how we treat our families. It permeates all politics, both national and religious. The degree to which we lust for power will determine how much sin we will commit to attain it.

Herod longed to be king. He went to Rome and bought the kingship of Judea. He had to spend three years warring to take his kingdom. He ruled about thirty-five years. He was known as Herod the Great—a great ruler in keeping order, a great builder whose work included the building of the temple in Jerusalem, and a great manager who at one time actually used his own resources to help the Jewish people in a famine. He did these good things to keep his power. But he did other things to protect his throne, too, like murder. He murdered his wife, his mother, and three of his own sons. Yet strangely enough, for religious reasons he refused to eat pork. This prompted Caesar Augustus to remark that it was safer to be Herod's pig than Herod's son. The pigs were no threat to his power.

Wealthy astrologers showed up in Jerusalem, asking, "Where is the one who has been born king of the Jews? We saw his star in the east, and we have come to worship him."

The words "King of the Jews" immediately gained Herod's attention and galvanized him into action. You see, "King of the Jews" was his title. When verse three declares he was disturbed, it is understating his agitation. He knew about the prophecy concerning a Messiah and called a meeting of the Sanhedrin to learn where the child was to be born.

The answer was found in Micah 5:2, "But you, Bethlehem Ephrathah, though you are small among the clans of Judah, out of you will come for me one who will be ruler over Israel." In Matthew 2:7, Herod calls the magi back to him. He sent them to Bethlehem, saying, "Go and make a careful search for the child. As soon as you find him, report to me, so that I too may go and worship him." When power is your great love, you may not be above using religion to accomplish your goals. His intent, declared the Scripture, was not to worship the Christ-child but to eliminate Him.

Herod is a picture of the love of power carried to its full potential for evil. While our own consciences would never allow us to go to the lengths of Herod to attain and protect power, there are some common denominators, some results of the love of power that can show up in most any of us.

The love of power destroys peace in our hearts. Several phrases in this section of Scripture give us hints about the state of mind of Herod. In verse three, we read that "he was disturbed." In verse eight, he is caught in a bald-faced lie. In verse sixteen, we read, "he was furious." In verse nineteen, we read that he died. In the face of an imagined threat to this throne, his reactions showed him to be totally devoid of inner peace or security. How many people are suffering, troubled, distressed, and disturbed at real or imagined threats to their power? What a tragic waste of precious life.

The love of power can distort people and events in our minds. We usually judge people by our standards. It's a terribly inaccurate manner of judging people, but most of us make the mistake of thinking others are like us. Herod loved power and couldn't imagine anyone loving anything else, so he completely misread the situation and the Christ-child. Therefore, he wanted to kill Jesus. Isn't that ironic? One of the main reasons Christ came was to die, and Herod's grandson would be part of the process when He did die. But Herod was so caught up in the love of power that he couldn't begin to understand the motives of someone given to the power of love.

Let's think about the ways of this world. Herod was exactly what the Scripture declares a one-world person will be. In the Word of God, the world is pictured as darkness and Christ is light. John called worldly or lost people "children of darkness" and followers of our Lord Christ "children of light." In John 3:19, we read, "This is the verdict: Light has come into the world, but men loved darkness instead of light because their deeds were evil."

This world is presently under the control of Satan. In John 14:30, Jesus called Satan the "prince of this world." When Jesus was tempted in the wilderness, Satan offered Jesus kingship of the world if He would worship him. The love of Satan's heart is power. He offered Christ power. The way of this world is power. The love of this world is power.

But it is not the way of Christ. One day, the power of Satan will be taken away, says the Book of Revelation. In the meantime, God is calling people through Christ to denounce the love of power and turn to the power of love. Because of the darkness of their hearts, too many are like Herod and afraid of the light. What a pitiful picture of misused human existence Herod was! It is one thing for a child to be afraid of the dark. It is something else for a grown man to be afraid of the light.

Now let's look at the power of love. Like the Ford Motor Company, God has a better idea. The love of power has progressed to the point where it is in danger of totally destroying our world. On a much closer level, how strange it is that we bring the world's model for power into the church or our homes.

Are you ready to listen to King Jesus? To Pilate, Jesus said, "My kingdom is not of this world."

"You are a king, then!" said Pilate.

Jesus replied, "You are right in saying I am a king. In fact, for this reason I was born, and for this I came into the world, to testify to the truth. Everyone on the side of truth listens to me."

Are you ready to listen to King Jesus? We know there's something different about this king when He declares, "I have come not to be served but to serve." Again, we hear Him say, "The greatest among you will be servant of all." "For God so loved the world that He gave His one and only Son."

Just before His crucifixion, He said to the leaders of His kingdom, "But you are not to be called 'Rabbi,' for you have only one Master and you are all brothers. And do not call anyone on earth 'father,' for you have one Father, and he is in heaven. Nor are you to be called 'teacher,' for you have one Teacher, the Christ. The greatest among you will be your servant. For whoever exalts himself will be humbled, and whoever humbles himself will be exalted," (Matthew 23:8–12).

Scriptures like these could fill a half-day's reading. Through His walk and talk, our Lord demonstrated and taught that His way is not the way of this world. Christmas may be an uneasy time for some, because it is the beginning of God's clear assault against the world's destructive love of power and His call to life abundant through the power of love. Most of human history is a portrayal of the failure of the love of power. If history tells us anything, it declares that love of power is not the answer.

Occasionally, there have been glimpses of the potential of the power of love. One such occasion was a cold night in 1915 on the western front during World War I. In one elongated trench were the Germans, and in the opposite trench were the British soldiers. From those trenches, they had been shooting at each other. It was bitterly cold, and there was snow. In both trenches, the men huddled together, trying to get warm. Overhead was the burst of guns and cannons. But as midnight on Christmas Eve approached, strangely the guns stopped.

From the German trenches there was singing, "*Stille nacht, heilige nacht, alles schlaft; einsam wacht....*"

Then from the British trenches there came "O little town of Bethlehem, how still we see thee lie...."

And the antiphonal singing continued from one trench to the other.

Suddenly, from the German trenches, the soldiers poured out

and raced across "no man's land." Ignoring the shouts of their officers, they ran to a place where just a few minutes earlier they would have met certain death. And the British troops poured out of their trenches. They met in no man's land, and they embraced each other. Now there was no sound of war just joking, laughter, and joy. For almost three hours, they fraternized. Repetitively, they made the statement, "Let the war stop. It's Christmas Eve!"

Our Lord told us that in this world we will continue to have wars. The love of power will plague human history to its end. But we can experience the power of love and its resulting peace in our hearts through Jesus Christ. That's why He came, to offer you and me the gift of Christmas, the gift of life, the power of love.

Chapter 7

When It's Time
to Leave the Huddle

Mark 9

Several years ago, Andy Griffith created no small stir in the entertainment world with a recording entitled, "What It Was, Was Football." He portrayed a "country boy come to town" who saw his first game of football. The field was seen as a "pretty little cow pasture" on which someone had planted posts and painted stripes. The game itself he described as "two bunches of men fighting over a little pumpkin." He concluded that the object of the game was to move that little pumpkin from one end of that cow pasture to the other without getting knocked down or stepping in something.

You and I have watched football, too, and we are aware that the huddle is not the most exciting part. Yet the huddle is very important to the team. That's when the assignments are made.

The ninth chapter of Mark records how one day Jesus took Peter, James, and John to the top of a mountain for a very special huddle. The Bible says that He was transformed or changed. The word literally means that His outward appearance reflected His inner nature. During that time, what He was really like on the inside showed on the outside.

Of course this made a deep and lasting impression on the apostles. John said in the first words of his Gospel, "We beheld His glory, the glory as of the only begotten of the Father, full of grace and truth," (John 1:14 KJV). Since He was full of God's grace and truth on the inside, that glory shone from His face and even reflected from His clothing.

To add to the frightening wondrousness of this great moment, Moses and Elijah appeared, and they talked at length with Christ. Don't you know our Lord was so very hungry for fellowship with folks like that? And He had missed it so much since coming to earth?

This time of talking among Moses, Elijah, and Jesus was interrupted by Simon Peter. Simon was so frightened that his mind was disengaged, his wits were frozen, but his mouth worked wondrously. He said, "Lord, this is what we're going to do. This is a beautiful place; we're having a great time here. Let's build three shelters, one for You, one for Moses, and one for Elijah."

Suddenly there was a cloud hanging overhead. This was a different kind of cloud. Instead of casting a shadow, it created light. From that cloud the voice of God interrupted Peter's interruption to say, "This is my dearly beloved Son. Listen to Him."

Just that quickly it was over. Peter, James, and John were lying prone on the ground, faces down and scared to death, afraid to look. Jesus bent down and touched them and said, "Don't be afraid, get up, it is time to go."

When they got to the valley, they found a scene of defeat and despair. A distraught father had brought his seriously ill son to be healed by the other nine apostles. They had been unable to do it and, gleefully, the Pharisees had seized upon this opportunity to discredit Christ and His message. Isn't that sad? Those supposedly religious people were delighted that the boy could not be healed.

Then the people looked up and saw Christ. Isn't it fantastic to know that in the difficult times we can look up and see Christ? He always comes down to the valley where there is need. What mixed emotions they had. They were ashamed for their failure, yet delighted to see Him. From this exciting story of contrasts between the mountain of inspiration and the valley of defeat, we learn when it's time to leave the huddle.

It is important that we get in the huddle. You're not even in the game if you're not in the huddle. The huddle is a time of information and inspiration and planning of strategy. We need these meetings of Christians together, away from the world.

It is interesting to note what Moses and Elijah and our Lord talked about. Do you ever listen to yourself and other people talk? Do it sometime. Very interesting. As we listen to what people talk about and combine that with what we know about heaven, I wonder if most people will have anything at all to say. It is highly unlikely that we will spend our time running down the administration. We won't be able to shake our heads and talk about how heaven is going to the dogs and how it used to be in the good old days. The weather will be perfect. We will not talk about our aches and pains because we won't have any. We shall not gossip or snipe at others because the Lord is going to remove that poison from our system. Well, take away gunning at the establishment, griping about the mess things are in, growling about the weather, groaning about our aches and pains, and gossiping about others, and you've just about eliminated the totality of some folk's conversational ability.

When we look at what these three men from heaven talked about, it will give us an idea of how conversation will go in heaven and also tell us what we ought to talk about in our Christian huddles here on earth. Luke 9:31 tells us that they spoke of Jesus' death on the cross. Have you noticed that is the thing most everyone in the Bible talked about? The cross and the resurrection are the theme of the Bible. Christ came to die for our sins and rose to prove His victory.

Moses and Elijah talked about the cross. John the Baptist said, "Behold the lamb of God, which taketh away the sins of the world." He was talking about Christ and the cross.

Isaiah prophesied, "He was wounded for our transgressions; He was bruised for our iniquities." John said, "The blood of Jesus Christ His Son cleanseth us from all sin."

Peter preached, "Ye were not redeemed with corruptible things, as silver and gold, but with the precious blood of Christ." Paul proclaimed, "God forbid that I should glory save in the cross of our Lord Jesus Christ." In the Revelation vision, John heard the cross as the theme of angels' song: "Worthy is the Lamb that was slain."

To talk of the cross is heavenly language. The old song should be our testimony. "I love to tell the story; twill be my theme in glory, to tell the old, old story of Jesus and His love." That's what we should talk about. It is not our lot to hang our heads and moan, "Look what the world is coming to." Rather it is our calling to proclaim, "Look Who has come to the world." When we are in the huddle, we should be preparing ourselves for the work God wants us to do. We should learn the assignments. Yet, instead of getting the assignment from our Lord, we are prone to spend our time telling the Lord what we want to do.

Peter is our prototype in this strange activity. During that high and splendid time of fellowship between Moses, Elijah, and Jesus, the Bible states that "Peter answered and said." But Peter was answering when he hadn't been asked. He was speaking when he had not been spoken to. And when he says, "Let us build three tabernacles," he was not asking for permission, he was telling the Lord what they were going to do. He was saying, "This is what we are going to do; this is a wonderful place. Let's stay on this mountain."

A while ago I said the old song, "I Love to Tell the Story," ought to hit at the heart of Christian conversation. Another "golden oldie" my mother said they always sang at the Sunday meeting at Spring Creek is entitled, "Beulah Land." The words: "I'm living on a mountain underneath a cloudless sky. I'm drinking from a fountain that never shall run dry. Far away the noise of strife upon my ears is falling, for I am dwelling in Beulah Land." From Simon Peter to now, the temptation of Christians is to find some place where they can retreat from the world and stay there, far away from the noise of strife. And we say, "Look, Lord, this is what we are going to do. Let's build a building here and we'll stay in this building. We will study how to witness, but we'll never leave the building to witness. We will read about what other missionaries are doing, but we will never be missionaries ourselves, because we'd have to leave the building. We will sit in our air-conditioned comfort and tell ourselves we are the only ones who care, but we will not go out into the world and tell the people who are hurting and sick and lost that we care. We are dwelling in Beulah Land."

But notice what happened. While Peter was talking, God stopped him and said, "This is my beloved Son. Don't tell him what you are going to do. Listen to Him and do what He tells you."

Then why don't we listen to Him? Our Lord's great instruction to His church is: "Go ye therefore and teach all nations, baptizing them in the name of the Father and the Son and the Holy Ghost: Teaching them to observe all things whatsoever I have commanded you." His very last words, just before the taxi-clouds took Him to heaven, were: "Ye shall receive power after that the Holy Ghost is come upon you, and ye shall be witnesses unto me." When we have come to the huddle, gotten our instructions, our inspiration, and the assurance of His power, then we are to run the play. Ignoring Peter's suggestion about the tabernacles and staying on the mountain, Jesus said: "Get up, it is time to go," and He led them down into the valley where people were needing Him.

An almost equal parallel in the life of our Lord preceded His death on the cross. He had taken these same three men into Gethsemane for a time of retreat and prayer. But after an hour He came, awoke His sleeping disciples and said, "Get up, it's time to go," and He went out and died on the cross for us.

Our Lord wants us to come to the meetings. Hebrews 10:25 commands us not to forsake the assembling of ourselves together. Huddles are important, but in the midst of the huddle we should hear Him say, "Come on, it's time to go run the play. Go tell the Good News." It is high time we Christians demonstrate to the world not only our enthusiasm and ability to hold great pep rallies, but our determination to get a good team on the field.

I must confess that I am a Dallas Cowboys football fan. For years I have lived and died with that team. For this reason, I will never forget that dreadful day of the 1967 National Football League Championship game, played up in the cold of Wisconsin. The field was frozen and slick. The temperature was below zero and our dear Cowboys had that championship snatched from their hands in the last seconds of the game. The last drive of the Packers presented a most impressive sight. With the clock running out, those Green Bay fans stood in that biting cold and, as with one huge voice, urged their team on, saying, "Go! Go! Go!" And they went, and won.

The eleventh chapter of Hebrews tells of past heroes of the faith: Moses, Enoch, Noah, Abraham, and many others. Then the twelfth chapter begins: "Wherefore seeing we also are compassed about with so great a cloud of witnesses, let us lay aside every weight, and the sin which doth so easily beset us, and let us run with patience the race that is set before us."

Do you catch the thrust of that? You and I are on the field, the only eligible team our Lord has now to use. And the grandstand is filled with the alumni, the faithful followers of our Lord in years past. There's Peter, James, Paul, John, Moses, Elijah, Noah, Abraham and scores of others who have served Him, and they are anxiously and tearfully shouting to us, "Go! Go! Go!" What a sin to stay in the huddle and lose the game by default!

Chapter 8

Fishing on the Right Side of the Boat

John 21:1–6

This episode is important because it is Scripture. But its importance to you and me is magnified because of its location in Scriptures–it is not just *that* we find it in the Bible, but *where* we find it. The account is set in the context of the resurrection of our Lord Christ. He is risen! What does that mean? To the disciples it meant that their relationship with Him was not ended. Their business with Him was not over. Their call was not revoked. Their purpose had become more power-packed and urgent than ever before.

In this exciting setting is an account of our crucified, buried, and resurrected Lord appearing to seven of His apostles. It is an actual account of an actual happening, but it is more. It is a parable to them and to you and to me. It has to do with their mission and ours. It asks the question, "Are you fishing on the right side of the boat?"

Here's how it happened. In the midst of their grief and confusion, Simon Peter and six others of the apostles were together. "I'm going out to fish," Simon Peter told them. And they said, "We'll go with you." So they went out and got into the boat. But that night they caught nothing.

Early in the morning Jesus stood on the shore but the disciples did not realize that it was Jesus. He called out to them, "Friends, have you any fish?" "No," they answered. He said, "Throw your net on the right side of the boat and you will find some." And when they did, they were unable to haul the net in because there were so many fish.

The question for us is, are we fishing on the right side of the boat? In our confused and self-destructive society, applications of this truth abound. To many living a frustrated and fruitless lifestyle, our Lord asks, "Have you caught anything? Have your efforts been satisfied?" And to our failure, He says, "You're fishing on the wrong side of the boat." Allow me to divert for only one application.

Our state needs improvement in its educational system. Our future is at stake. I support and congratulate our governor in his effort to bring better education to our people. Yet in fishing for ways to finance the program, we are in danger of fishing on the wrong side of the boat and coming up with very empty nets.

A lottery is not the way to go. Gambling is not an economically sound way to support any program. Senator Alexander Wiley has rightly said that the idea that gambling will be a revenue raiser is an illusion. Every dollar raised will require several dollars more spent in higher police costs, higher court costs, higher penitentiary costs, and higher welfare and relief costs. Gambling produces no new wealth, provides no useful service. It drains the salaries, savings, and investments of a community into a business enterprise that serves no human need.

There is evidence that gambling is not a socially sound way to go. The crime rate in gambling states is much higher than in non-gambling states. USA Today recently devoted an entire editorial page to the fact that compulsive gambling is a disease reaching epidemic proportions in our land. We say we want to help the people of our state. If we create new gamblers, we create new losers. We are told that we are the least educated and poorest state. If we allow gambling interests to take advantage of our ignorance, they will create a deeper poverty.

I think that diversion is apropos, but it is a diversion from the main thrust of this text. I didn't resign my citizenship when I became a preacher, and I want to say that. But the main thought of our text is missions, our purpose as a church of our Lord Christ.

In order to point us to that purpose, that calling, our Lord asked, "Are you fishing on the right side of the boat?" Fishing on the right side of the boat means that we are fishing. In his book *The Salty Tang*, Frederick Speakman tells of a little old lady who was by no means the typical cartoon of the American tourist. She carried no camera, her hat was shapeless, and her wallpaper-patterned dress, though clean, looked like it might have been slept in. You and I, after a few exchanges with her, would have been able to round out

her story: a mid-American grandmother who had always longed for this trip abroad and whose children were now staking her to it. She had tried to crowd an unconscionable itinerary into too few days but she was certainly going to see Westminster Abbey. The guide was accustomed to all the tourist types, from the gushing romantics to the California belittlers, but he couldn't get the wavelength of this little soul. This Whistler's mother had springs in her heels and from one spot of interest to the next kept leading him rather than being led, listening to every word of his droning description but with never a comment. She glanced at every stone and symbol and inscription with the steady eyes of hungry interest, yet silently conveyed the idea that she wasn't about to be impressed. And when she at last spoke, it was to break into his pattern with a question that left the guide slack-jawed and puzzled. With one quick gesture, she swept Westminster Abbey, that citadel of church tradition, that rich storehouse of historic greatness, and said, "Young man, young man, stop your chatter and tell me, has anyone been saved here lately?"

That question must keep coming up. When we meet together in this beautiful structure, and we are so very grateful for it, we must ask: "Has anyone been saved here lately?"

When we are numbering our attendance and count the dollars donated, knowing these are pretty fair indicators in our world of how we are doing, they are a long sea mile from the main thing. The real question is, has anyone been saved here lately?

Life as a Southern Baptist has its downs in recent years. We've discovered the Pharisees among us who are more anxious to follow the letter of the law than its spirit. Jesus said to a like group, "But you have neglected the most important matters of the Law—justice, mercy, and faithfulness. You strain out a gnat and swallow a camel." We've strained brothers' and sisters' agreement with our ideas and interpretations while swallowing the whole grotesque and ugly camel of power politics. Someone would be asking, "Has anyone been saved here lately?"

Fishing on the right side of the boat means we are fishing according to His direction. So often we fish our own way. After all, we say, we're fishing. We try our schemes. We borrow schemes

from other churches who caught some fish. That's often like getting a blood transfusion from someone with a different blood type. We try to run the church like the world around us. Some of the most secular books I've read have been on the subject of church growth. Adopting the standards and techniques of the world around us assures us we will forfeit our opportunity to change our world.

We need desperately to learn the lesson of this simple story. Their nets were empty when they fished their way, but when they followed His simple instructions, the nets were bulging. There is available for our enjoyment a beautiful rhythm of life. It is the rhythm of obedience and blessing. How many of us have ignored and failed? We work hard, we stretch and strain, we burn the midnight oil. We may work hard at making our class, our department, our church a success, but the net comes up empty.

Then we hear Him say, "Cast the net on the other side." What do we say, "Lord, I've been a port side fisherman all my life. Don't expect me to change to the starboard now"? I've been doing it this way all my life. I'm a port side, left-handed fisherman, and that's just the way I am. "Cast the net on the other side." And when we do it, the net is full. Success. We've learned one of life's largest lessons: The secret of life's rhythm, the wonderful cycle of obedience and blessing.

Baseball has been a love of my life, especially growing up. I played at every opportunity. I didn't play all that well, but I played often. I was a line drive hitter—I hit a lot of line drives to the catcher! Baseball taught me a unique lesson. When you go up to bat, you are in close proximity to people who are not interested in your success. The pitcher and the catcher are dead set against your succeeding, and the umpire doesn't care whether you succeed or not.

Also, you are being told things and advised from two dugouts. On one side is the opposing team's dugout. They say strange things to you. They plant false and negative thoughts in your mind. They suggest that the pitcher, who throws the ball 100 miles per hour, might be a little wild and has a propensity to stick the baseball in the batter's ears. This is bad enough now, but I played baseball awhile ago, just as the earth's crust was cooling, and we did not have

batting helmets.

On the other side, equally distantly removed, was my team's dugout. They told me I could do it (though I seldom did). They told me I was the man for the job, that the pitcher had a rag arm, that his elevator didn't go all the way to the top, and that I could handle with ease any pitch he offered. From my dugout came not only encouragement but valuable information. Instructions like: "Hit the ball behind the batter." "Bunt." "Let the pitch go" so the base runner could steal second base. I learned soon that if I and my team were to succeed, I had to listen to the right dugout.

If our enterprise for Christ is to succeed, we must listen to our Lord. We must fish from the right side of the boat. He told His church to go and make disciples, but He didn't just leave it at that. First, He said, "Pray, pray, pray until my Spirit comes upon you." If they had just heard the Great Commission and immediately devised a plan to storm the world, they would have failed. They would have worked hard, fished hard, and caught nothing. But they learned to listen to our Lord. They learned to fish from the right side of the boat.

Even when we know what to do and are determined to do the good thing, if we set out to do it in our own strength and in our own way, we are doomed for disappointment. We finally hear the agonizing words: "Fellows, have you caught anything?" Then we hear the call: "Cast your net on the right side of the boat." And we learn to pray, to seek His way, to submit to Him and we experience the beautiful rhythm of successful living, the rhythm of obedience and blessing.

When we are fishing on the right side of the boat, we are fishing with a net. When you fish with a net, you are not selective as to the kind of fish you catch. We are fishing on the wrong side of the boat when we cast about in a lost world with specialized lures designed to catch a particular kind of fish.

John 21:11 declares: "Simon Peter climbed aboard and dragged the net ashore. It was full of large fish, 153, but even with so many the net was not torn." Biblical commentators suggest that the 153 was not the total number of fish caught but the number of different kinds of fish caught, thus fulfilling the prophesy of Ezekiel 47:10.

Greek zoologists of the day identified 153 kinds of fish in existence. In this way, Jesus was declaring the "catch" was to be the people of the whole world. To cast our net under His supervision means that we will abundantly reach all people.

The church is not the country club at prayer. Someone may ask, is this a white person's church? Yes. Is this a black person's church? Yes. Is this an Asian person's church? Yes. Is this a Hispanic person's church? Yes. Is this an Indian person's church? Yes. Is this a rich person's church? Yes. Is this a poor person's church? Yes. Is this a church for someone in the middle of the economic ladder? Yes. Is this a children's church? Yes. Is this a young person's church? Yes. Is this a single adult's church? Yes. Is this a married couple's church? Yes. Is this for someone in their middle years? Yes. Is this for someone in their older years? Yes. Is this a family church? Yes. Is this a handicapped person's church? Yes.

The church is a family of faith, a family of God's people, a family of the Father who repeatedly has said, "There is no difference," and "Whosoever will may come." We must understand our Lord's use of the term *fishing* to mean not the taking of lives but rather a rescue mission. The church of Jesus Christ is on a rescue mission. If we are church, we will have a rescue mentality.

I heard many years ago about a town on the shore of a great sea where there was a group of good people who were disturbed that so many were dying in shipwrecks just a few miles out to sea. Determined to do something about it, they organized themselves and called their organization the Lifesaving Society. Pooling their scant resources, they were able to buy some boats and build a little shack stocked with cots, a stove, and some blankets. When a storm came up and passing ships got caught in the reefs and were breaking up, they would get in their small boats, go out into the sea, rescue the shipwrecked people, and bring them back where they could be treated. It wasn't long until this unselfish bravery was heralded all over the land. People began to send money to help in the work, and many wanted to join the Lifesaving Society. With their new wealth and new members, they erected a beautiful building. Experts were hired to come and lecture about the techniques of lifesaving. With such wonderful facilities and instruction, they stayed around

the building most of the time and talked about lifesaving. They didn't go out to sea much anymore. They just played games and heard lectures in the safety of their building, feeling very noble about being a member of the Lifesaving Society, while out in the sea people were dying with no one to help.

We need to be fishing. That is our responsibility. We need to do it as He directs. And we must want to reach all the people He loves.

Chapter 9

Is God Calling You?

Genesis 15:1

Have you ever been scared? I don't mean frightened; I mean scared. And did your fear come after the thing that scared you was past?

Coming into my hometown from the direction of Tonk Valley, there was a double curve down a grade that dropped about thirty feet. It was a rugged little stretch of road. By mountain people's standards, it was tame. By Texas standards, it was steep and treacherous. In 1953, when gasoline was twenty-nine cents a gallon, automobiles had big V-8 engines and much higher centers of gravity. Many more cars per capita rolled over then than now. Four of us were returning from a church league softball game at Tonk Valley, and we came into that treacherous stretch of two-lane highway at an unacceptable rate of speed. While our softball playing had not been too swift, our pace of travel was. We suddenly found ourselves going downhill almost out of control, trying not to roll over while barely keeping the car out of the deep ditches on either side of the road. Strangely enough, this activity occupied our minds so much that no fear set in during the ride. But when we got to the bottom and coasted the car to a stop, we all seemed to lose the blood in our faces, and one the food in his stomach. I looked at my hands and they were shaking. All of this came after the danger was over.

In chapter 14 of Genesis, we learn that Abram had taken a small force of well-trained men, followed an army all the way past Damascus, and routed the army in a daring nighttime raid, rescued the people they had captured, and recovered the goods they had stolen.

When he was back home, the fear set in. He may have thought, "What have I done? I have made five kings my enemies. While my men surprised and routed them, they have the power to come against me and strongly defeat me."

Our text, in Genesis 15:1, states: "After this, the word of the LORD came to Abram in a vision. 'Do not be afraid, Abram. I am your shield, your very great reward.' "

Is there any fear in your heart? Are you afraid of dying? Or living? Afraid you don't have what it takes to face what you have to face? Afraid you have blown it? Have you just come down some emotional or physical Tonk Valley road experience, and you are frightened because you now realize how vulnerable your life is? Then you too can hear God's call. "Don't be afraid. I am your shield, your very great reward."

The Word of the Lord came to Abram in a vision. It was a personal word. It came "to Abram." This is the fifth time in these first fifteen chapters of Scripture that God has spoken a personal word to someone. Is it possible He can speak a personal word to you? This word came to Abram in a vision. This is the first time in the Bible that someone gets a word from God in a vision. If you get a word from God, how will it come?

Hebrews 1:1–2 tells us: "In the past God spoke to our forefathers through the prophets at many times and in various ways, but in these last days He has spoken to us by His Son."

The first verb "God spoke to our forefathers" is the Greek verb *lalasus*, "He spoke." It's a progressive past, a process in which He reveals Himself bit by bit to the forefathers.

For "But in these last days He has spoken" the verb form is *elalasen*, which means the process is completed. It is not to continue. The last word has been spoken. The final word is given. Does this mean you won't get a word from God? No. On the contrary, it means you and I can get the final, completed, the last word from God. The final completed word comes to us through Jesus Christ.

In Matthew 11:27, our Lord Christ said that all things come through Him, that everything He has comes from God. And verse 28 says He chooses to reveal Himself to you. "Come unto me, all ye that labor and are heavy laden, and I will give you rest," (KJV). Do you have trouble believing the Bible? Come to Christ. Meet the author, and then you will love His book.

"He who comes to me, I will in no wise cast out" says Christ. Come to Him for your word from God. And what is that word? "Don't be afraid." This is based on a decision. Abram, we are told in the last verses of chapter 14, had decided not to be identified with the wickedness of Sodom, and he had decided to be wholly identified with the Lord God. He demonstrated this in his public declaration of identifying with God, and in the giving of a tithe.

When you and I repent, turn away from the sin of this world and identify, turn to Jesus Christ as Savior and Lord, then we too will have the personal word from our Lord God. "Don't be afraid. I am your shield."

"I am your shield." What does that mean? That He will protect; that God is our bodyguard. Yes, it means that, but it means much more. It also means that we operate under the authority and power of God, and therefore we have His authority and power. When a soldier carried a shield in a battle, he was not only carrying a defensive weapon, he was carrying his identity. The shield was emblazoned with the crest of his king. It means he represented that king and therefore had the power of the kingdom behind him.

Because Abram identified with most high God, he had the power of most high God with him. When you and I submit with faith and love to our Lord Jesus Christ, then we take into our lives the power and privilege of the Kingdom of God.

Do you remember when Jesus met the Roman centurion whose much-loved servant was seriously ill (Matthew 8)? The Roman army captain said, "Lord, I do not deserve to have you come under my roof. But just say the word, and my servant will be healed. For I myself am a man under authority, with soldiers under me. I tell this one 'go' and he goes; and that one 'come' and he comes. I say to my servant 'do this' and he does it." Jesus was astonished and said to His followers, "I tell you the truth. I have not found anyone in Israel with such great faith."

What did that Gentile, professional soldier understand about faith that is so vital? He understood that you have whatever power you submit yourself to. He was under the authority of Rome. So when he commanded his men, he spoke with the authority of Rome. He knew Jesus was under the authority of His Father, so He possessed the power of His Father.

Most high God was saying to Abram, "Don't be afraid. I am your God. I am your protector and your power."

Now the personal word tells of a personal reward. "I am your shield and your very great reward." "I am your reward," says God. Not "I will give you your reward," but "I am your very great reward."

We begin with substandard notions of our Christian faith. We approach God like little children interested in what He's going to give us. We begin by being preoccupied with the gifts of the lover and fail to see the greatest thing of all is the love of the giver. As we mature in this life, we learn that we didn't need our parents' gifts nearly so much as we needed our parents. As we grow in faith we learn our greatest reward is our wonderful Heavenly Father Himself.

The largest tragedy of the televangelists scandal is not the embarrassment it brought to our cause, large as that is. The greatest tragedy is the heretical teachings of those fallen angels. Each built his empire on a health-and-wealth platform, saying, "Love God and He'll make you rich. Have faith and you'll never be sick." Now, He is a God who gives some the power to get wealth. He is a God who heals. But His greatest gift to us is Himself.

I saw a wonderful Christian friend lose his fortune of four million dollars overnight because of the criminal acts of a trusted partner. But the light in his eyes didn't go out. Rather it blazed brighter. He said, "I lost the money, but I have the Father and He is more real to me than ever."

Others might look and mock and say, "Hey, Christian, what's the use in all that church going and Sunday school teaching and tithing? You've lost everything." And his reply was, "God Himself is my very great reward."

I think sometimes our Lord calls His weakest vessels to be pastors. We have to spend hours in His Word. And we meet people who keep demonstrating in all conditions that what we say is true.

How often I visit with someone who has been given some news that would crush a one-world person, only to see the light of God flash in their eyes. Fortune may be gone. Health may be gone. Death may be near. "But I have God," they say.

What is the use of faith? What is the reward of coming to God through Christ? It is His call to you: "Don't be afraid. When I am your shield, I will be your very great reward." Isn't it true we're all headed to a time when whatever things we think we own will be gone? In terms of eternity, all of us are bankrupt. One day it will all be gone. In terms of eternity, all of us are terminally ill. We will not live forever. If we have the Father, we have everything. If we do not have the Father, we have nothing.

There was once an extremely talented young baritone. He was a sensation on the New York stage and radio programs. He was weighing the choice between signing a lucrative contract with the opera or becoming the soloist for a virtually unknown itinerant evangelist. During this time he found some words on the music holder of his piano. He wrote the music to accompany those words. His name was George Beverly Shea. The young, unknown itinerant evangelist was Billy Graham. These are the words Bev Shea matched his music and his life to:

I'd rather have Jesus than silver or gold;
I'd rather be His than have riches untold.
I'd rather have Jesus than anything
This world affords today.

Than to be the king of a vast domain
And be held in sin's dread sway.
I'd rather have Jesus than anything
This world affords today.

God is calling you. He is saying, "You don't have to be afraid. If you will make me your shield, I will be your very great reward."

Apparently government-guaranteed security is not a guarantee of personal happiness and fulfillment.

One could call the roll of all systems of government: monarchy (government by one), oligarchy (government by the few), plutocracy (government by the rich), aristocracy (government by the best). Democracy, government of the people, by the people, and for the people, is the best governmental system in this world!

This fact must be taught. We are not born automatically believing anything. Young people today need to be told they will probably live thirty years longer because they were born here instead of in India. They must be taught that we are only one-sixth of the world's population, yet control one-half of its wealth. They do not think of how this system has provided the freedom for its citizens to become the healthiest and best educated people of the world. So we must tell them.

Dr. Kenneth McFarland had spoken to the town forum in Tulsa, Oklahoma. After the meeting a young man rushed toward him. His eyes showed his rage. Blood vessels stood out on his tense neck. He was clutching a newspaper that pictured a map pointing out the pockets of poverty in this nation. "You didn't say anything about that, did you? You didn't say what this so-called wonderful American system has done for those people!"

"Son," he replied, "Do you think all the people who started this country were wealthy? There was a time when ninety-nine percent of all the people in this nation were poor. Most of them indentured themselves into slavery just to pay the passage to get over here. There has been nothing to compare in history with how these people used this system's opportunity to lift themselves higher and higher under the protection of God and the American flag. We're not through yet. Let's do more, but let's thank God for the opportunity we have."

The young man's expression changed. He softened. "I want to see you again," he said. "Rather, I want you to see me again. When you see me the next time, I'll look different. I'll be different." Many of our radical young people would be different if we had just done a better job of teaching Americanism.

As we encourage ourselves in the midst of our difficulties, we must also be warned. I am convinced we can apply the words of God through Amos to His nation as the Word of God to our nation. "I have loved you. I have chosen you. I have blessed you."

Scholars are now taking a new look at political democracy and are saying, "It must be emphasized that Christianity is not dependent upon democracy, but there is considerable evidence that democracy is dependent upon Christianity. As the principles of Christianity diminish among the people so does the effectiveness of democracy diminish."

History's trash basket is lettered with the ruins of nations who thought they could never fall. Almost every nation that has gone down in defeat has cried, even as it died, "It cannot happen to us." This was true of the Egyptians, the Babylonians, the Persians, the Greeks, the Syrians, the Jews, and the Romans. It was true of France and Germany. And for years, in spite of the sobering facts of history, America has been saying, "It cannot happen to us."

As best we can tell, this assertion is based upon two conclusions: One, America is superior from a standpoint of inventive genius; and two, God is on our side.

We have learned lately that we are not the only ones who can invent. We have also learned that inventive genius can find a cure for polio but not for the poisonous disease of hate. We have discovered that inventive genius can produce power, but it cannot produce peace. It can land on the surface of the moon, but it cannot explore a person's heart. We have faced the stark realization that the mysteries of outer space are nothing to be compared to the mysteries of inner space, the guilt-ridden, confused, tangled, empty emotions of modern man. Our great problems are not from without but from within. The harder crisis in this country is not economic or political but moral and spiritual.

We know a country's safeguard is not in commerce, or Tyre would never have fallen; not in art, or Greece would never have fallen; not in political organization, or Rome would never have fallen; not in military might, or Germany would never have fallen; not in religious ritualism, or Jerusalem would never have fallen; not in treachery, or Japan would never have fallen. The time may soon be coming when it may be said of America: "A nation's safeguard is not in her inventive genius, or America would never have fallen." A country's safeguard is in obedience to the commands of God.

God has blessed this nation so we could be a blessing to the world. How many are the chances we've had to send our sons and daughters overseas with bread and Bibles, but we would not pay the price in money or concern because of our selfishness? So we had to send our sons with bayonets and bombs, and many of them never came back. We have been blessed with greater prosperity and power than any other people in any day in history; but instead of the goodness of God producing integrity, it too often has produced immorality. Instead of producing love, it produced lust. Instead of devotion, it produced drunkenness.

Hear Him say in Amos 3:2–3, "I have chosen you, blessed you, that is why I must punish you all the more for your sins. For how can we walk together with your sins between us?" The reason for God's judgment is spoken in verse 10: "My people have forgotten what it means to do right."

I don't know the dean of students at Arizona State University, but I'd like to. I think he must be a great man for this is what he said: "It's awful what we've been doing. We've been telling people that nothing is for sure. Everything is relative. Nothing's entirely right, nothing's entirely wrong; nothing's black, nothing's white, everything is gray. We've been telling them anything is all right if enough people in a given area at a given time think it is. We've been sending people out with all sorts of situation ethics. We've been sending them out on the stormiest sea of life we've ever known, and we've been sending them out there with no compass, no anchors, no fixed stars to steer by. And we wonder why they're floundering. We wonder why they're sinking. We wonder why they're going down. We're going to have to return to a thing we understood in this country at one time, and that is that some things are forever right and some things are forever wrong and never the twain shall meet."

It is a time for us to demand the same honesty of ourselves as we do of our government. A government represents and reflects its people. If we grow up a generation of young people who lie, cheat, and steal their education, you can expect nothing else but that they will lie, cheat, and steal in business or government in later years.

When I was in college, they told us there would be no professor in the room with us during testing times because we had an "honor system." I asked an upperclassman what they meant and he said, "It means they've got the honor and we've got the system." Anyone or any nation operating like that is doomed to failure.

There is a well-traveled tale of an extremely wealthy man who, in his last days, called for his son, his only heir, and said, "Son, it looks like I'll be gone soon. I have left everything to you in my will. The homes, the stocks and bonds, the land, it will all be yours." Then he seemed to be going rapidly, and the son leaned over and said, "Dad, is there anything I can do for you?" He said, "Yes, take your foot off the oxygen hose."

It is high time in America that we say to the pushers of immorality, who tell us we don't have to be honest, that we don't have to keep our marriage vows or any others; to the peddlers of smut and obscenity, those who try to poison our minds; to those who would poison our bodies with liquor and other drugs; to all who care not one whit what they do to people, just so they get their money; it is time we say to that breed of vipers who influence this nation to do wrong, "Take your dirty foot off the oxygen hose! You're killing this country!"

Amos tells us that when we sin against God, we sin against a God of love and we sin against a God of judgment. If we refuse to obey His commands and live in His love, we will have to face the consequences of His judgment. Proverbs 14:34 tells us: "Righteousness exalteth a nation, but sin is a reproach to any people" (KJV).

In every warning from God, there is encouragement. The Great Physician never diagnoses a case without prescribing the cure. All the harsh warnings of the book of Amos are given to set the stage for four words found in chapter five and verse four: "Seek me and live!" When that happens, God can bless America again.

Chapter 11

Raising Cain

Genesis 4:1–9

There are quite a few people who believe that environment has a great deal to do with crime and with wrongdoing, with evil in our world. Years ago, when I graduated from college, the speaker at the graduation exercises told us about Saint Theresa being sent by Saint Peter from heaven to look over things. After her first week in the United States she called heaven and said, "Hello, Saint Peter, this is Saint Theresa. I have bad news to report. Things are not good here in New York City. I'll call you again next week from Chicago."

She called from Chicago. She said, "Hello, Saint Peter, this is Saint Theresa. I'm making my report to you and I'll give it to you better in writing, but things are not looking good here. I'll call you next week from Las Vegas."

The next week the phone in heaven rang. She said, "Hello, Saint Peter, this is Saint Theresa. I've found that the further West I get the more deteriorated things are. I'll call you next week from Los Angeles."

The next week the phone in heaven didn't ring. The third week the phone rang and she said, "Hello, Peter, darling. This is Terry."

Well, the first sin took place not in the slum but in a paradise where everything was perfect. And the first murder took place on the way home from church. Adam lay with his wife, Eve, and she conceived and gave birth to Cain. She said, "With the help of the Lord, I have brought forth a man." Later she gave birth to his brother, Abel.

Now Abel kept flocks and Cain worked the soil. In the course of time, Cain brought some of the fruits of the soil as an offering to the Lord, but Abel brought fat portions of some of the firstborn of his flock. The Lord looked with favor on Abel and his offering. But on Cain and his offering, He did not look with favor. Cain was very angry. His face was downcast. Then the Lord said to Cain, "Why are you angry? Why is your face downcast? If you do what is right, will you not be accepted? But if you do not do what is right, sin is crouching at your door; it desires to have you, but you must master it." And on the way home from church, Cain attacked and killed his brother, Abel.

A lot of sad things happen around church and in church. During this time of the year, we are starting to hear again the rhetoric that has to do with our own Southern Baptist controversy.

A friend of mine called the other day to say, "Why don't you get in the game?" And I said, "My friend, that's not the game. That's the fight underneath the stands. That's the brawl going on among the bullies, not the game. The game God has given us is to go into the world and make disciples. The game for Southern Baptists is to support and undergird the way of training and equipping people to go into all the world, and supporting the 6,000 missionaries we have. The game is to give integrity to the gospel of Jesus Christ and not to embarrass it."

Our Lord tells us in the Sermon on the Mount to out-live and out-love the world around us with integrity, to make sure the gospel has His realness to the world about it. That's the game. And so I would say to my friend and to all Southern Baptists, "Why don't you get out of the fight and get into the game?"

Well, this passage is about the first family. You remember that was a very interesting family, Adam and Eve. Adam was the first man to say to his wife, "You're the only one for me," and she knew he meant it. How drastically their lives changed after the great mistake they made. It would be called today a functional disorder. Adam lost his job and had to move. The new work and life was painful and difficult. Soon a baby was on the way. This had never happened before. There was no doctor, of course, to see. No manuals to read; they just lived the experience. And because things had been going so badly since they malfunctioned in Eden, they were delighted with the new child. Gratefully, Eve named him Cain.

But as the boy began to grow, it was apparent he was more the son of his mother and dad than he was of God. And he became as much a problem to them as they had been to their Heavenly Father. Raising Cain was not a pleasant experience.

I'm sure as a teenager he was bored. Wouldn't you be bored?

How boring a life that must have been. He was angry. He could look into that beautiful Garden of Eden and see all the beauty and all the good life, all the paradise lost, and I'm sure he thought it was terribly unfair of God to keep him out of there. After all, he didn't eat the forbidden fruit. His parents did. He didn't ask to be born. Why should God keep him out? "I wouldn't blow it like they did," he probably thought.

Seeing that angel guarding the gate, keeping him out of the garden, probably angered him greatly. I can imagine a few times he tried to slip into the garden. Don't you? There were no circuses, no movies, and no ball parks to slip into. They probably tried to slip into Eden. Of course, he didn't make it. But we can surmise that Eve and Adam had some difficulties raising Cain because we can compare the birth announcements.

Would you look there in the latter part of verse 1? When Cain was born, Eve said, "With the help of the Lord I've brought forth a man." Verse 2 says later she gave birth to his brother Abel. You get the idea that the first experience was kind of bad. They weren't all that excited when the second child came along.

Now, raising Cain was not easy. And on a day when Cain and Abel went to church, they brought an offering. It was unthinkable to come before God without an offering. Worship always involved giving in the Word of God. But we read that Cain brought some of the fruits of the soil as an offering to the Lord, and Abel brought fat portions of the firstborn. Some of the fruits of the soil are contrasted to some of the fattest calves of the firstborn. It's evident that Abel took his offering business much more seriously than Cain. The Word says that the Lord looked with favor on Abel and his offering. But on Cain and his offering, He did not look with favor. Interesting.

It is not the offering alone that God's concerned about, but with the person bringing it. The kind of person whose worship to God involves simply *some* of what he has is contrasted with the one who gives the fattest ones of the firstborn of what he has. He doesn't wait to see if there's enough left over after he's paid all his expenses to make an offering to God. He gives of the firstborn.

Cain was sulking. He was angry with God's reaction to him and his offering. He probably thought God should have been thrilled that he showed up and that he brought any offering at all.

When we are faced with an inadequate worship of God, when the offering is not acceptable because the offer-er is not right, then God speaks His words of warning. He speaks His warning in love. He always does it in love, but it is a word of warning.

It isn't hard to detect how Cain reacted to this warning. This was a call for a changed heart. And this man in his inner conflict knew in his heart that it was he who was wrong. God wasn't his problem. Neither was the brother who had done the right thing.

His problem was pride. Pride says, "You can't apologize. You cannot admit that you're wrong. What would people think? You're just emotionally upset. It'll pass and then you won't feel this way. You won't feel like you're wrong again."

Tell me. What happens when you stand in the presence of the white heat and the white light of God's holiness? Other people stood in this same presence of God. Moses did. And he took off his shoes because the ground was holy.

Isaiah stood that day and realized for the first time that he was in the presence of God, even though he'd been to church a lot of times before. And getting his glimpse of God, he said, "Woe is me. I am a man of unclean lips."

John the Baptist was preaching righteousness and baptizing people because they were sinners, and he said to the Lord, "I need to be baptized by you." Simon Peter one day said, "Lord, depart from me. I am a sinful man. I don't deserve to be in your presence." And so he humbled himself before the Lord God.

But Cain had no room for anyone in his heart but Cain, and because of that God warned him of something. And then we read the saddest word in the Bible. Have you ever wondered what is the saddest word in all the Bible? This is the first time it appears. It's not the first time it happens, but it's the first time the word appears. And this is a harder word than *death* or *hell*. It's the word *depart*. It is the saddest word in the Bible. It is the mother of sorrows; it's the fountain of woes.

Lost is a sad word, but why are people lost? *Death* is a sad word, but why is there death? The Bible says we're lost because of sin and that we are dead in trespasses. Since we are dead spiritually, we die physically because of sin. The wages of sin is death.

The Lord said to Cain, "Because you have sinned, sin is crouching at your door. It's a wild animal that will not be satisfied with this one sin but will bring more." It's a picture of this wild animal waiting to pounce on you. He said, "It desires to have you. It is your self that is at stake, Cain."

Oh, it is all right in the stewardship of life and things and possessions that we look after the things we have. But, my soul, how careless we are often in looking after ourselves. You who are too old to try to protect what you have and leave yourselves wide open to the devil: Sin is crouching at your door. It wants you to commit one sin and then when you do that, you invite another. And when we commit one sin, we have invited a horrible thing which is right at our door. Every sin we commit has its consequences. Every action has its reaction. Every deed has the thing it causes. We sow what we have reaped as we reap what we have sowed.

As we make our bed we lie in it. As we sin, we make another burden. Because sin brings with it another wilder, larger, stronger beast crouching at the door blocking the way to God and waiting to pounce upon us.

Sin keeps multiplying, keeps getting worse. The grand larcenist began as a petty thief. The rapist began with his pornography. The murderer here began with his anger and resentment and hatred. The cycle is vicious and it grows larger.

There is another word, and it is a word of love. It is a word of encouragement, but it sounds like a cruel word. Hear it: "but you must master it." "It desires to have you but you must master it." Oh, can a leopard change his spots? Can a sinner stop sinning? Our sins are stronger than we are. In this world of empty, windy-word preachers, don't read to me empty and windy words of awe. Go make yourself clean. These are cruel words. You *must* master it.

But you understand these are the words from God, and God knows us. He knows what we can do, and He knows what He can do in us. And you and I may ask someone to do something impossible but our Lord God will not. For He knows what is impossible; He knows what is possible; He knows what He can do in you.

And so these are words of invitation. They are "welcome" words.

He said, "If you do right [and that means if you come to Him], will you not be accepted?" The word *accepted* means to be lifted up. He said, "Cain, you can't really be raised. You can be raised to the level of acceptance in my own heart. You can be raised, Cain, by the power of Christ."

In the words of God, there is a connection made between the blood of Abel and the blood of Christ. In Hebrews 12:24, "To Jesus, the mediator of a new covenant, and to the sprinkled blood that speaks a better word than the blood of Abel." The better word is the word *pardon*. The blood of Abel called for revenge. The blood of Christ calls for pardon.

Chapter 12

Who's to Blame?

Genesis 3:10–13

When things go wrong, when you go wrong, do you try to place the blame somewhere other than on yourself? An up-to-date revision of an old adage might state, "It matters not whether you win or lose but where you place the blame."

Hardy Denham, a good friend and able preacher, has declared the most popular game in our nation to be the "blame game." Indeed it is. It is a favorite indoor and outdoor sport. Any number of people can participate. It's as old as Eden and as new as this morning's paper.

R. G. Lee said in his inimitable style several years ago, "An alibi is an anesthetic that a coward administers to himself in the presence of a painful or difficult duty." All through the Bible we find people playing the blame game.

The oldest book in the world is probably the book of Job. It concerns a man who was as good as a person could be. A series of calamities drastically changed his life. His wealth was stolen by thieves and destroyed by nature. His children died in a freak accident. He became seriously ill. While sitting in the midst of his agonies, some friends came to visit. They said, "Job, it's got to be your fault."

The apostles saw a man blind from birth and they asked, "Lord, who's to blame, this man or his parents?"

Lazarus, a close friend of Jesus, died. Four days later our Lord arrived at his house and Lazarus' grieving sister Martha greeted Christ with the words: "If you had been here this would not have happened," as if to say, "It's your fault."

At the most crucial hour in history, Jesus Christ stood before Pontius Pilate, who alone had the legal right to pronounce the death sentence. Though he knew it was wrong, Pilate let them kill our Lord. But he played the blame game. He washed his hands in water and said, "I am innocent of the blood of this just person," as if he was telling the crowd, "It's your fault, not mine."

The first blame game was played in the Garden of Eden. Caught red-handed in direct disobedience, a panicky Adam blamed both God and Eve. Eve blamed the serpent. Neither of them blamed themselves. When the delicious apple of life has gone sour, whom do you blame? Do you blame God? Adam did.

I remember in my childhood that I was normally thrilled to see my father coming home, but sometimes just the opposite was true. Some wrong I had done or work I had not done was to be faced. On those evenings I did not run to him; my impulse was to run *from* him. Such an evening had come for Adam and Eve. In the past they had joyously fellowshipped with the Father, but on this day, in shame and fear, they hid. When quizzed by God as to the cause of the sudden ruinous, rupture of relationship, Adam answered, "The woman you put here with me—she gave me some fruit from the tree, and I ate it." He seemed to be saying, "God, it's your fault. You are responsible. If you hadn't given me that woman, this dumb thing would never have happened."

Stephanie Powers suffered the loss of two of her closest friends within hours. William Holden, intoxicated, fell in his apartment, cut his head, and bled to death. Natalie Wood, intoxicated, slipped from her boat and drowned. Ms. Powers asked a reporter what many misguided and unthinking people have asked: "How can a loving God do a thing like this?"

You remember, don't you, what insurance companies call natural catastrophes? That's right—"an act of God." Tornadoes, hurricanes, and floods are called "acts of God." Many people call whatever terrible thing that happens "an act of God." They remind me of the oft-repeated story of the little boy telling his friend how he drowned the cat. "I dumped him under the water and held him a long time. When I brought him up, he was sputtering and spewing. Then I dumped him again and I held him there." At this point, the boy realized the preacher was overhearing this sordid conversation, so he added, "and the Lord took him."

Know this for sure: You are wrong to blame God. He is not to be blamed for wrong. Adam was wrong to do it, and so are we. It is true that the Lord God allows evil to exist in this world, but allowing evil to exist and willing it to exist are two different things. Our Lord will allow any prodigal among us to rebel, run to a far country, and ruin his life, but He will never push us out of the house. James wrote, "Let no man say when he is tempted, I am tempted of God: for God cannot be tempted with evil, neither tempteth he any man" (1:13). The meaning is clear: the Lord God is not to be blamed when things go wrong in life.

A great young couple in a church where I was pastor faced one of life's largest lumps. Their three-year-old child was killed in an accident caused by a drunken driver. In the immediate hours after the calamity, I heard no less than three well-meaning people piously intone that this was God's will. At the funeral, I said, "This is not God's will. The God you and I worship does not go around taking the lives of little children. This was caused by someone other than God. But in His love, God says: 'I will not let death have the last word for your baby. She is alive. She is with me and one day you will see her again.'"

And just as God is not praised for all the good He does, He also is blamed for many things He does not do. You are wrong to blame God. Well, who else can we blame? You guessed it, we can blame others.

It is very true that, just as others are involved in helping us do good, other people can help us do bad. Responsible and accountable is that one who encourages you to take the first drink, to do the first dope, to steal the first thing, to cheat on the first test, to tell the first lie, or to take whatever exit ramp from the freeway of right living you were induced to take.

However, though one who involves you in wrongdoing is responsible, to blame others for your mistake is a mistake.

Eve did indeed offer Adam the apple. She may have even suggested things would go better in their relationship if he ate it, but it was not good for Adam to blame her for what he did. We must not blame others because God's Word clearly declares it to be sin. When you blame others, you are playing God. The first five verses of Matthew 7 declare you have neither knowledge nor insight to judge another human being.

Beware of the sin of fault-finding. In all candor, I must say this is probably the worst sin of those who think they are the best people. We ministers can be terribly guilty here. Jesus told about a Pharisee, a professional religious person, who was so in the habit of fault-finding he even ran down people in his prayers. He paraded proudly before God all his good virtues and then he said, "I thank you, God, that I am not like that miserable fellow standing over there!"

Yet the worst sins in this world are not committed by the bad people. The worst sins are of disposition, which poisons the streams of life. Sins against human happiness are the hardest for our Lord God to stomach. Yet how many Christians are fault-finders, unofficial, unqualified fruit testers in the kingdom of God. If there was an Olympic event for long jumping to false conclusions, they would set world records daily.

You and I are not God. We must not blame others. Of course, when we blame others we are really trying to excuse ourselves. People who attempt to excuse themselves are not usually good at it, but they can be fascinatingly creative.

From an automobile association comes a list of statements given by people involved in accidents. One man wrote, "A pedestrian hit me and went under my car." Listen to this one: "Coming home I drove into the wrong driveway and collided with a tree I don't have." Still another said, "I collided with a stationary bus coming the wrong way." A man who may represent the true feelings of a lot of us asserted, "I consider that neither of us was to blame but if either was to blame, it was the other one." When we blame others, we are attempting to shift the guilt from ourselves to them. It is like sending someone else to see the doctor when you are ill. If we can't blame God and we can't blame others, who is left to blame?

That's right. True release and healing is begun when we adopt the attitude of the spiritual songwriter, "Not my brother nor my sister but it's me, O Lord, standing in the need of prayer."

Adam took the fruit and ate it. Eve did not put it in his mouth, work his jaws, or swallow it for him. Adam tried to shift blame to Eve. "This woman you gave me, she gave me of the tree." But his last words were more true than he intended, "And I did eat." Remember the words of Shakespeare put into the mouth of Cassius: "The fault, dear Brutus, is not in our stars, but in ourselves."

Do you realize what good news I'm giving you? In most cases, if you don't like the way your life is going, you have direct and ready access to the one who is responsible.

The prodigal son realized that. Here he was in economic depression in a foreign land, broke, living with the pigs. What did he do? Blame God? No, God did not put him there. Did he blame a nebulous thing called society and the government? No, it wouldn't have changed a thing. Did he blame his high-living friends who helped put him there? It would not have made any difference. But the Bible says: "He came to himself." He got to the real root of the problem. "He came to himself and he said, 'I will arise, I will go to my father and I will say I have sinned.'"

At this point, our loving Father, our gracious Lord, said if you are willing to take the blame, you don't have to keep it. He will take the blame for you. Listen to Him: "'Come now, let us reason together,' says the LORD. 'Though your sins are like scarlet, they shall be as white as snow; though they are red as crimson, they shall be like wool'" (Isaiah 1:18).

David said, "Then I acknowledged my sin to you, and did not cover up my iniquity. I said, 'I will confess my transgressions to the LORD'—and you forgave the guilt of my sin" (Psalm 32:5).

John wrote, "If we confess our sins, he is faithful and just and will forgive us our sins and purify us from all unrighteousness" (1 John 1:9).

In teaching as adjunct faculty member at Southern Seminary, I enjoyed the company of a man I've admired a long time. He is Dr. Carl Bates, an outstanding preacher of the Word of God. I told him about working on this sermon, studying this particular passage of Scripture. He shared with me a word of testimony. These are not his exact words, but this is his story. "At about age 17, 18, or 19," he said, "I was struggling with guilt and confusion in my life. There were wild horses inside me, leading me to conduct that I knew was wrong. Yet I had great difficulty handling them. I was an unconverted church member. I had forgotten the ethics. I knew what was right, but I didn't have the dynamic, the power to live well. In my confusion and frustration," he continued, "I built a case against God. I said, 'God, it's your fault. I didn't ask to be born. I didn't decide to look like I do or be what I am. All the wild horses raging in me are your creations. I am what you caused, not me.' "

"And God said, 'I accept the responsibility of making you and risking what you can be, and on the cross I took the blame for all your mistakes. If you'll come to me, I'll take your blame away and in addition, I'll give you my life.' "

Dear friends, you only compound your sin when you blame God. You only make yourself miserable when you blame others. Because of Christ, as you accept God's forgiveness in Him, you can even stop blaming yourself.

Chapter 13

The Word of God Forever

1 Peter 1:22–25

Every year in Jackson, Mississippi, there is an arts festival. It is a time set aside to honor arts and artists. There are concerts, ballets, displays of arts and crafts, and tours of beautiful homes and buildings. In 1976, David Roddy, our church's educational director, decided we ought to have a Bible Day during the arts festival. Collections of rare and expensive Bibles were brought to our church and displayed. The mayor designated that Sunday as Bible Day in Jackson. That morning I preached about the miraculous way God has preserved His Word against physical and intellectual attacks. On Monday I was called by the executive director of an Honor Society for Junior College Students in America. She told me her organization was bringing together their most brilliant students for a survival conference. She said scientists and environmentalists were being brought in to discuss the chances of the survival of life on earth. "I was driving through Jackson yesterday," she said, "and I heard your sermon on the survival of the Word of God and I want you to come and deliver that sermon at our meeting."

Well, I did and I shall forever remember the experience. Every person on that program painted a picture of despair. Together they presented a collage of calamity: overpopulation will choke the world, there will be no room; starvation will be common, there will be no food; living will not be possible because there will be neither air nor water.

After hours of that, how strange it must have sounded when I read to them: "The Word of the Lord endures forever." The Good News states that it is not just the Word of God that shall endure forever, but those who link their lives by faith to the living Word will live forever also. The message of our text is that the enduring Word imparts enduring life to all who will receive it. God has preserved and forever will preserve His Word. He has preserved it because through the Word He offers His love, Himself, His life to all people.

All through the ages, enemies of our Lord have tried to eliminate the Bible but to no avail. Let's review some of the attacks that have been made upon the Word of God and be encouraged by the victorious survival of God's Word in each instance.

There have been three kinds of attacks: attempts to destroy it physically, attempts to keep it from being understood, and attempts to discredit it intellectually. The Word of God has successfully withstood every attempt to destroy it physically. The Bible has a record of survival so miraculous it can only be explained as divine providence. There has never been a time when it has not met opposition of some kind. History has proven it will not drown. It will not burn. It will not be torn asunder. A divine power protects it and promotes it. Millions of copies have been put to flame, thrown to the fish, cut to pieces, and otherwise destroyed, but this Bible is indestructible. Like the mythical Hydra of old with nine heads, any of which when cut away was replaced by two others, the Bible has multiplied with every assault upon it.

About 600 B.C., Johoiakim, king of Judah, attempted to destroy the Word of God and failed (Jeremiah 36). He was angered at the message that the scroll of Jeremiah contained, so he cut it to pieces and threw them into the fire. But the Word did not burn, only the paper on which it was written. The writing was reproduced at the command of God. Today we have it in the book of Jeremiah. So it has always been. The efforts of men and devils to annihilate the Word have brought about its sure increase. The ashes of its burning are the seeds of reproduction.

In 303 A.D., the Roman Emperor Diocletian instigated the most terrific onslaught against the Bible the world has ever known. Every manuscript that could be found was destroyed. Every copy of any portion of the Bible that could be located was burned. Thousands upon thousands of persons who possessed copies, and even their families, were martyred. After two years of ruthless slaughter and destruction, a column of victory was erected over the embers of a Bible with the inscription "Extinct Is the Name of Christians." Less than three years later, in 312, the Emperor Constantine declared the Bible to be the Word of truth. Desiring to place copies of the New

Testament in all the churches of his empire, Constantine offered a reward to anyone who could discover and deliver to his officers the Holy Book. Within four hours, fifty copies were brought out of hiding and presented to the emperor.

> They burned truth in the marketplace
> And thought their work complete.
> But next day with a smiling face
> They met it on the street.
> They threw it in a dungeon damp
> And thought it was no more
> But lo it walked with lighted lamp
> Among them as before.
> They scorned and ostracized it
> And ordered it to depart.
> But still it dwelt in all the land
> And challenged every heart.

Now think of how the Bible has survived in understandable existence. You know the Bible was written in Hebrew and Greek. When the prophets of the Old Testament and the apostles of the New Testament lived, no one had ever heard of English. Every time we read an English Bible we ought to be supremely grateful for all the sacrifice that is involved in our having it. Circumstances surrounding the first English translation of the Scriptures form an exciting chapter in the history of the Bible.

In 405, Jerome, the great Christian scholar, completed a Latin translation of the Bible from Greek and Hebrew. For this he was bitterly assailed by the bishops of his time. He was accused of tampering with the Word of God and promoting his own ideas, a reward many translators have received since his day. But Jerome's version lived through the Dark Ages as the Bible of Europe.

In 1379, Dr. John Wycliffe gathered about him a group of Oxford scholars and with them began the translation of the Latin Bible into English. His commitment to be a tool of God, to give His Word to the people, cost him severely. It cost him his job, his freedom, and finally his life.

William Tyndale is responsible for the first printed English Bible. He was hunted down, captured, strangled, and burned at the stake for the crime of printing and distributing the Word of God. His last words were: "Lord, open the king of England's eyes."

His prayer was speedily answered. In less than three years, Henry VIII authorized the publication of the Great Bible, the combined work of Tyndale and Miles Coverdale, whose translation appeared in 1535. At least one copy was chained in every church in England so that all the people might read.

Another attack that has been leveled against the Word of God through the ages is an intellectual attack. One such onslaught was made by the French philosopher Voltaire and it splendidly illustrates how vain it is to struggle against the Word, and also what a great sense of humor our Lord God has! Voltaire dared to predict that within 100 years the Bible would be a forgotten book. These are his words: "One hundred years from my day there will not be a Bible in the earth except one that is looked upon by an antiquarian curiosity seeker." Before the century was up, his very home was owned and used by the Geneva Bible Society, from which millions of Bibles have been sent around the world. One hundred years after Voltaire's prediction, a first edition of Voltaire's work sold in the market in Paris for $11 and on that identical day, the British government paid the Czar of Russia $500,000 for the Codex Sinaiticus, a copy of the Bible.

Robert Ingersol, a noted American agnostic of the 19th century, once held a Bible high in his hand and presumptuously declared: "In fifteen years I will have this book in the morgue." In fifteen years Robert Ingersol was in the morgue. The Bible was as much alive as ever.

Have you heard this?

Last eve I paused beside the blacksmith's door
And heard the anvil ring the vesper chime;
When looking in, I saw upon the floor
Old hammers, worn with beating years of time.

"How many anvils have you had," said I,
"To wear and batter all these hammers so?"
"Just one," said he; and then with twinkling eye,
"The anvil wears the hammers out, you know."

And so, I thought, the anvil of God's Word
For ages skeptic blows have beat upon.
Yet, though the noise of falling blows was heard
The anvil is unharmed—the hammers gone.
—Attributed to John Clifford

The Word of God endures forever, declares 1 Peter 1:25, because it is "the word which by the gospel is preached unto you," (KJV). May I address you who are called to preach just a moment? Isn't it great to be a preacher? Aren't you glad God called you to share the gospel? Almost all of us recall the days when we began to realize He was calling us to this wonderful task. Like you, I had said, "Lord, I am yours. I will marry whom you want me to marry. I will live where you want me to live. I will do whatever you want me to do. Lead me, Lord, help me want for my life what you want." Then I began to dream, while sleeping, about being a preacher. I thought, "Lord, that's too good to be true. Are you really going to let me be a preacher?"

Being called to preach means you are a preacher for the same reason Kermit is a frog, and Moby Dick is a whale! You can't help it! A preacher preaches God's Word for the same reason a bird flies in God's sky. It's what you were born to do. It's what you were created for!

Our text declares, it is the Word which by the gospel is preached. Without this Word, the gospel is not preached. The term, "biblical preaching" is a redundancy. It's like saying "two twins" or "honest truth." Preaching must come from the Word or it is not preaching; it is only speech-making. A preacher must love the Word. He must handle it with the same awe with which some people handle diamonds. He must treasure it in the same way some people treasure money. It is the Word of God forever, and from it we preach the gospel.

Why has this Word survived? Because God wants us to hear the gospel. For in it He confronts us with our sins and calls us to life. God's Word is alive because in it the disease of our soul is diagnosed. Our Creator confronts us in His Word with what we already know. Something is wrong. We say, "Oh, God, what's wrong with us?" His answer is in Romans 3:23, "For all have sinned, and come short of the glory of God," (KJV). Our next question is obvious and natural. "Lord, is sin serious? Is it a bad disease?" Sadly He gives the hard news of our true condition. "For the wages of sin is death." But, as though He just can't wait to say it, He adds to that sentence, "But the gift of God is eternal life through Jesus Christ our Lord!" (Romans 6:23 KJV).

Here is what the Word of God is all about. God wants us to know Him, so He spoke a Word. Not a Word in a language that only some people could understand. In the beginning verses of John's Gospel, we read: "In the beginning was the Word, and the Word was with God, and the Word was God.... And the Word was made flesh and dwelt among us."

God wants us to know Him—not just His will, or He would have simply handed us the law. Not just His power, or He would have merely displayed it in nature. Not just His love for beauty, or He could have given us a rose or the song of a bird. Remember what Jesus prayed in John 17:3? "And this is life eternal, that they might know thee the only true God, and Jesus Christ, whom thou hast sent," (KJV).

In the Bible we meet Christ and therefore we meet God. The Bible is the Word of God because there is a voice behind the Bible, which speaks. That voice is the voice of Christ. Through Christ, God is saying I love you. He didn't just stay in heaven and say I love you. He came here and became one of us and proved His love for us. Do you catch the thrust of that? The Great Physician made a house call! He didn't simply reply to our sinful condition by advising: "Take two doses of hope and I will see you at ten o'clock on judgment day." No, by His birth and life He identified with us. By His death He sacrificed himself for our sins. By His resurrection He won the victory over death for us. The message of the Bible is Jesus Christ saying to one and all, "Come unto me, all ye that labour and are heavy laden, and I will give you rest."

The Word of God will endure forever, and so will you if you know Him, the Living Word, Jesus Christ.

In the last paragraph of the Sermon on the Mount, our Lord said, "Therefore whosoever heareth these sayings of mine, and doeth them, I will liken him unto a wise man, which built his house on a rock: And the rain descended, and the floods came, and the winds blew, and beat upon that house; and it fell not: for it was founded upon a rock. And every one that heareth these sayings of mine, and doeth them not, shall be likened unto a foolish man, which built his house upon the sand: And the rain descended, and the floods came, and the winds blew, and beat upon that house; and it fell: and great was the fall of it" (Matthew 7:24–27).

There were two houses and one storm. The question is not if you will face the storms and ravages of time, but if you will still be standing when they are over. If you are founded on the Word of Christ, you will stand. "The word of the Lord endureth forever." And because of that, so can you!

Chapter 14

Integrity

Genesis 39

If it fell your lot to choose a person to fill the most important position of leadership in your land, what kind of person would you look for? If somehow it became your responsibility to be that person, what characteristic, what personal character trait would you pray for?

I think the word to describe what would be needed is *integrity*. Basically, the word means wholeness. In mathematics, an integer is a number that isn't divided into fractions. Just so, a man of integrity isn't divided against himself. He doesn't think one thing and say another, so it's virtually impossible for him to lie. He doesn't believe one thing and do another, so he's not in conflict with his own principles. It's the absence of inner warfare that gives one an extra energy of clarity of thought.

The most beautiful thing about God's revelation is the wonderful way He dresses His truth in personality. In twelve chapters of Genesis, He lines out in unmistakable clarity what integrity looks like. Integrity lived in a man names Joseph, whom God used to save several nations from starvation.

Joseph, like many great men, did not have an impressive family background. In fact, it was underwhelming. His grandfather, Laban, and his father, Jacob, were known as the slickest, underhandedest dealers in the east. Neither was a man you would ever buy a used camel from. Joseph watched the relationship between his father and grandfather totally deteriorate. He experienced his father's stressful flight from the anger of Laban straight into a confrontation with Esau, the brother he had cheated. Esau had made a vow to kill Jacob. Perhaps it was in the context of that dilemma, seeing what problems his mother's trickery had caused, that Joseph decided that honesty was the best policy, perhaps the only one if you want to survive.

There were some positive experiences on that trip. Joseph watched his father come back from a midnight encounter with

God. He walked with a limp, but he was changed in other ways too. He was humble and strong and confident. He had been changed by the living God.

Joseph saw another wonderful thing on that trip. He saw his uncle Esau do a totally unexpected, unnatural thing. He welcomed, accepted, and forgave the brother who had cheated him out of his birthright. In Genesis 33 we read of the meeting of those two brothers. Esau said in effect, "I don't want revenge. I don't want you to make amends. I don't want any of your goods. I just want to be your brother." In return, Jacob said, "Esau, your face looks to me like the face of God."

How could the face of hairy Esau look like God's face? It was the face of love and kindness and forgiveness, and that does look like the face of God. I'm sure little Joseph never forgot that confrontation.

The next time we see Joseph, he is seventeen years old, spoiled and rotten and arrogant. He is obviously favored by his father, and he flaunts that relationship before his older brothers. He angers the whole family by telling of dreams in which they all bow down to worship him. And he runs to his father with news of every bad thing he sees his brothers doing. None of the above endears him to those brothers. At the first opportunity, they try to kill Joseph, but their entrepreneurial nature instead prompts them to sell him as a slave to some Egyptian merchants. Thus, at seventeen, Joseph faces the cruel test of adversity. He is separated from his father, his security. He becomes a slave in Egypt.

In Egypt he is sold to a man named Potiphar. Yet even in slavery he prospers. After ten years, we find him thriving as a trusted steward, the manager of all Potiphar's property. Having weathered well this first test of adversity, he faces the test of allurement. By now Joseph is twenty-seven years old. Genesis 39:6 states he was "well built and handsome." If you're reading the King James Version, it says he was a "goodly person and well favored." That means well built and handsome.

These attributes of this Hebrew Robert Redford did not escape the lustful eye of Mrs. Potiphar. The sin she suggested to him was not all that uncommon in Egyptian society. For ten years, Joseph had been away from any moral teaching, yet he resisted day after day and steadfastly declared he could not betray his master or sin against his God. For this he was tragically rewarded. The spurned woman spread lies and soon Joseph found himself in prison.

Some of God's great people have faced this kind of adversity. What a splendid opportunity to throw up your hands in despair or clench your fists in resentment and ponder what kind of mad dog world this is which attacks the innocent.

By God's grace, Paul and Silas, in a Philippian jail, turned a raw deal into a revival. In an even greater display of faith, Joseph weathered this trial of adversity for three years. Then he faced the biggest trial of all—the trial of success.

Success has ruined more people than failure. Joseph handled success, too. In a bizarre and divinely directed turn of events, Joseph was named governor over all of Egypt, second in command only to the Pharaoh. Genesis 41:43 asserts that Joseph was given the chariot of the second in command, sort of an ancient Egyptian counterpart of Air Force II. And wherever he went people were commanded to kneel down. Joseph handled well his advancement.

The time eventually came when his brothers were totally at his mercy. He could have done with them anything he pleased. Yet his forgiving spirit was like that of his uncle Esau's all those years before. What a whole person! What a man of integrity!

If Kipling hadn't addressed these words to his son, we would believe he was describing Joseph.

If you can keep your head when all about you
Are losing theirs and blaming it on you;
If you can trust yourself when all men doubt you
But make allowance for their doubting too,
If you can wait and not be tired by waiting,
Or being lied about, don't deal in lies,
Or being hated, don't give way to hating,
And yet don't look too good, nor talk too wise:

If you can dream—and not make dreams your master;
If you can think—and not make thoughts your aim;
If you can meet with Triumph and Disaster

And treat those two impostors just the same;
If you can bear to hear the truth you've spoken
Twisted by knaves to make a trap for fools,
Or watch the things you gave your life to, broken,
And stoop and build 'em up with worn-out tools;

If you can talk with crowds and keep your virtue,
Or walk with kings—nor lose the common touch;
If neither foes nor loving friends can hurt you;
If all men count with you, but none too much;
If you can fill the unforgiving minute
With sixty seconds' worth of distance run;
Yours is the Earth and everything that's in it,
And—which is more—you'll be a Man, my son!

That poem is entitled "If" and admittedly those are awfully big "ifs." But Joseph did it. He was able to keep his head, to wait for God's plan to jell. He was lied about, hated, yet did not return lies or resort to hating. He dreamed big dreams, yet was not destroyed when life seemed headed in another direction. He faced the direst disaster and the highest triumph and did not lose his integrity to either. He lived up to the best in himself.

Many are the people who ignore the best in themselves and surrender to the worst in themselves. He had a highly developed sense of honor. He knew that some things are forever right and some things are forever wrong, no matter if you are in Egypt where they don't live like that. He had a conscience and listened to it. Instead of suppressing his conscience, he obeyed it. That made him a powerful man. He had the courage of his convictions. There is no more powerful a person to be found than that one who knows he is right.

Someone has observed that those who ultimately succeed, those whose lives make a difference, are those who are driven by an obedience to the unenforceable. They do right no matter what others do. They do more than they are expected to do. They are obedient to that which is unenforceable.

Would you like to be a person of integrity, a whole person,

undivided? You can. The secret is spelled out four times in Genesis 39. In verse 2, "And the LORD was with Joseph." In verse 3, "And his master saw that the LORD was with him." In verse 21, "But the LORD was with Joseph." And in verse 23, "The LORD was with him."

You want to be a whole person? Come to God through faith in Jesus Christ, and the Lord will be with you. In fact, He says, "I'll never leave you nor forsake you." How we need people of integrity today! Do you want to do the best thing for your family, for your country, for your state, for your city? Don't criticize. You don't have to criticize. Become a better person. Let Jesus Christ rule your life. He'll put it all together and you'll be one person, undivided.

Chapter 15

God's Recycling Plan

Luke 15

Jesus' enemies were always eager to use whatever cannon fodder they could find to blast criticism at Him. When they saw some notorious sinners and dishonest tax collectors coming to hear His sermons and then actually taking Him to lunch, they smiled their sardonic smile and said, "You can always tell what a person is like by the kind of company he keeps!"

Well, that is a half-truth. God's Word does indeed warn us to watch the company we keep. In 2 Timothy 3:2–5 we read: "For men will be lovers of self, lovers of money, boastful, arrogant, revilers, disobedient to parents, ungrateful, unholy, unloving, irreconcilable, malicious gossips, without self-control, brutal, haters of good, treacherous, reckless, conceited, lovers of pleasure rather than lovers of God, holding to a form of godliness, although they have denied its power; Avoid such men as these," (NAS).

But there is another sense in which you cannot and must not judge a person by the company he keeps. This is when his commitment to serving others places him in their midst.

Would you say a doctor is sick because he associates with sick people? Or a funeral director is dead because he is constantly in the presence of the deceased? Or a kindergarten teacher is ignorant because she spends hours with people who cannot read? Neither could you say that Christ was sinful because He ministered to sinful people.

On another occasion when this same bunch of religious snipers made this criticism, our Lord displayed a sharp sense of sacred sarcasm. "A doctor does not spend his time with those who are well, but with the sick."

This time, however, He responded by telling three stories related to one theme: the loss and recovery of a sheep, a coin, and a son. The heart of God, He is saying, does not give up on you no matter how "lost" you get. Like the sheep, you may wander away;

or like the coin, be lost by neglect; or like the son, demand your due and stomp off into a far country. No matter what you've done or where you are, the Father is anxious to have you back, to let you know your place in His mansion and as His son is ready and waiting for you.

But the story does not stop there, nor should we. In our eagerness to edit the Bible, we are prone to leave off at the place where the house on the hill is jumping with merriment and the senses of sound and smell are simultaneously tickled by the waves of happy music and the scent of barbecued beef.

In hearing the tale of the other prodigal, the older brother, those first century religious critics knew that Christ had turned their words back at them. "You criticize me for being with sinners," He said, "helping them find their way back to the Father's house. I criticize you for not doing that, for assuming that faith in God is to be greedily grasped and hoarded rather than shared with people who need it."

They perceived what many a present-day believer needs to see. They were the elder son in that story, the man who stayed in the father's house, worked on the father's farm, performed what he deemed the necessary duties, yet strayed farther from his father's heart, love, and concern.

Jesus is saying some things to them and to us through these stories. He is actually telling us why more Christians sign up for softball than for visitation, and why the hardest thing to promote in anyone's church is a witnessing program. He points out the misconceptions that lead us to blindly think we are rendering our best service when we show up, yet He constantly admonishes all Christians to reach out.

Luke 15 declares that three factors that must be present before lives can be reclaimed for Jesus. The first is this: we will never reach a soul for Jesus unless we first know that soul is lost. No diligent search is made for anything without first becoming aware that it is missing: The shepherd looked for the sheep because he knew it was lost. The woman would not have "swept the house," looking for the coin, if she had not known it was lost. The father would not have spent those long, hard, sad days gazing down the road if he had not known the condition of his son.

The most difficult truth to dispense today is that people really are lost without Christ. It is easier to recognize the "lostness" of some things than others. Any good sheepherder who can count can tell when a sheep is missing. It doesn't take an audit by a CPA for a housewife to know she's lost the grocery money.

But how can you tell when a person is lost? "Lost" for the livestock and coins is simply a matter of geography; they are out of place. "Lost" for someone made in God's image is much more complex. It means he is out of fellowship with his Creator. There is a gnawing hunger in his heart. There is a haunting knowledge that life ought to be much better. There is a gradual or abrupt erosion of character and a gnawing dread of death. This world is quick to suspect that there are hypocritical people hiding behind masks of religion, yet a far greater number are sad, empty, lost people hiding behind masks of artificially-induced happiness.

We must return to a basic gospel truth: Anyone without Christ not only has eternity's hell waiting *there*, but is actually experiencing the worst possible existence *here*. This is why Paul called the Ephesian Christians to remember how before Christ they were "dead" in trespasses and sins.

If you believe the Bible is the Word of God, if you believe Jesus Christ spoke truth, then you must believe that your neighbor, though he may be socially correct, personally magnetic, financially solvent, and morally acceptable, is a lost soul if he does not know Jesus Christ. Jesus said, "I am the way and the truth and the life. No one comes to the Father except through me."

Only as you accept that truth will you understand why Jesus spent so much time with people so unlike Himself. You will never understand God's love nor your Christian purpose in life without understanding this foundational fact. We will not look for them until we know they are lost.

Another thing: we will not look until we care that they are lost.

Have you wondered why our Lord told the stories of the lost coin and the lost sheep when the story of the prodigal son alone is so searching and revealing and profound? I think He is pointing out our sinful sense of values.

Have you had much experience with people who raise livestock? I have been asked on several occasions to jump in a pickup and go with a man to feed his cows. "Won't take twenty minutes," he would say. But when a cow or calf came up missing, we drove for hours through muddy pastures searching for that animal. "He may be caught in barbed wire," said the obviously worried rancher, "or be sick." And so everything else, including my work, was forgotten until we found that cow. Yet that same rancher, a Sunday school teacher, when asked about members of his class, had no idea what may have happened to them.

The sad, sad thing about these three accounts is that the only thing not looked-for was the son. The shepherd looked until he had found the sheep. The woman looked until she recovered her money. But the older brother, who knew where his brother was, who knew how his father's heart was broken and how his father longed to have his brother back, would not go look for him because he just did not care. He did not share his father's love.

Dr. Charles Jarvis is a great speaker from San Marcos, Texas. Besides his DDS degree, he also holds an engineering degree. That is proper, he says, "because dentists do build bridges." He tells of an experience in his life to which we can all relate.

A thirty-nine-year-old friend died suddenly and without warning one night. "If you love them, tell them," he pleads. "I waited too long. I know what's eating me up and I don't want that to happen to you. It's a guilt complex that's eating inside of me saying, 'You muffed it, brother. You were with him all the time and you muffed every opportunity you had to tell him how much you care for him. Now you can't.'"

In his grief, Dr. Jarvis wrote these lines:

Life's a trial and life's a worry.
Life's a problem; life's a hurry.
Life's a busy, crowded way;
Good intentions go astray.
I had a friend the other day,
I haven't now 'cause he passed away.

I meant to write, to phone, to call,
But he didn't hear from me at all.
I only hope that he can see now
What his friendship meant to me.
Life's a busy, crowded way.
Good intentions gone astray.

Jesus' life as well as His teaching demonstrates this third fact: If you know they are lost and if you care that they are lost, then you will do something about it.

There is no mistaking the intentions of our Lord for His church's mission. A careful reading of the New Testament reveals not one instance of our Lord telling the world to go to church. But there are repeated commands to the church to go to the world with the gospel.

"Go and make disciples of all nations."

"Be my witnesses in Jerusalem, Judea, Samaria, and unto the uttermost parts of the earth," He commanded.

"Follow me and I will make you fishers of men," He invited. And those men who had been going where the fish were to be caught followed Him down the dusty, crowded streets where people were to be found.

Jesus talked of a field "white unto harvest." It takes no agricultural genius to reason that you can't reap a harvest by hanging around the barn. You have to go out into the field where the harvest is.

All too many Christians are like the cowboy from around San Antonio who took a train trip to New York City. When he returned, some of his friends asked how he liked the city. "I never saw it," he said, "There was so blamed much going on around the depot."

Every now and then someone says, "I just don't want to be pushy. Religion is such a private thing." Well, that is like a doctor seeing the signs of critical illness in a friend and saying, "I won't tell him. I won't try to save his life. I don't want to be pushy."

It is strange to hear a citizen of this country talk about their hesitancy to go out and try to sell something. Why, this land has gotten its prosperity because of aggressive salesmanship. The more I study our economic system, the more convinced I am that someday we will lift the salesman to a much higher position of social honor than we have. If salesmen stop selling, our whole economic pipeline will clog up and stop all the way back to the field and the factory.

In Disneyland they have Main Street USA, a main street just like it was in 1900, with horse-drawn fire wagons and horse-drawn streetcars. Do you realize that everything we have gotten to improve on that was brought to town by a salesman? You know that the City Council did not all of a sudden decide to buy a red fire truck. No. A salesman brought one to town and the council turned him down. "People like to see the horses run," they said. Of course, the horses never got the firefighters there in time to save the house. But the salesman kept coming back and finally the City Council decided to buy a fire truck by a 5–4 vote.

All I'm saying is this: Our country has prospered not just because we've produced better things, but because we've had people to aggressively tell us about those better things.

It used to bother me when people called me a salesman for the Lord. It doesn't bother me anymore. This word tells you and me that it is not enough to know Jesus Christ died on the cross to pay for our sins, and that anyone who will can know fellowship with Him forever. It becomes our responsibility to go and tell. If we know they are lost, and if we care that they are lost, then we are going to do something about it.

Chapter 16

Good Faith, Bad Faith

Genesis 15:6

Because of your commitment to foreign missions and reflections of that in our Lottie Moon Christmas Offering and the Cooperative Program, I was invited to attend this past week's meeting of the Foreign Mission Board in Richmond, Virginia.

Between here and Atlanta, I shared a three-seat row in a plane with a bright young man from Baton Rouge on his way back to his army unit in Berlin. We discovered in each other a kindred faith. After deplaning, we were walking down the hallway of the crowded Atlanta terminal when he said: "Wait a minute! I want to give you something!" He stopped and put his bag on the floor, opened it, rummaged around in it and gave me this. It's a piece of concrete. Looks like it could have come from the curb in front of our house. "It's a piece of the Berlin Wall," he said. And suddenly that chunk of concrete became valuable to me.

It is now part of my trophy case. My trophy case only has two things in it—this rock and this trophy. I won this trophy at our church's golf tournament this year. It reads: "Over Fifty, Right-Handed Pastor Division, First Place." Now that's a rare trophy. How many right-handed pastors over fifty do you know who can shoot 102 in a golf tournament and get a trophy for it? Now this trophy is real. I was there.

But I got to thinking about that rock. How do I know the young army officer was telling the truth? How do I know this rock didn't come from a sidewalk in Baton Rouge?

This thought caused me to remember a story about NASA giving moon rocks to universities geological departments of study. Well, for some reason, the geology department of one school was overlooked and when they complained, there were no more rocks left. So the NASA people went out into a pasture and picked up a rock and sent it to the university. In several weeks the university's head of the school of geology called a press conference and announced, somewhat sarcastically, "We now have documented proof that the cow really did jump over the moon!"

How do I know this rock is from the Berlin Wall? I have to trust the young man who gave it to me.

Disturbing, isn't it, that we have to live by faith? And that our life, our liberty, our welfare, and our eternity are vastly affected by what or whom we choose to believe.

The atheist chooses to believe there is no God and he, she and all who trust them are eternally affected. Adolph Hitler believed in a strategy as strongly as any one can. He caused others to believe in him, and World War II and its ravages resulted.

At the same time across the world, Hirohito believed himself a deity, and his nation followed him in faith to its own defeat.

Saddam Hussein believes; he has faith in an imagined god of destruction, murder, and conquest. All the world today is affected by his faith and the millions who follow his faith.

There is good faith and bad faith. Faith is a powerful thing. Therefore, the direction we aim our faith, the thing we believe and follow, has in it seeds of ruin or reward, of hurt or harvest, of good or tragic bad.

Abram had faith. It was good faith. It was faith that resulted in the blessing of God coming to the world. Through Abram and His seed, God sent His Word, His love, His purpose, and His Son to save this world.

One day, God began to tell Abram again of impossible things He would do through him. In the midst of God's conversation with Abram, we are given a sort of editorial insertion. In the midst of these promises the writer of Genesis states "And Abram believed the LORD."

"Abram believed the LORD." Faith in faith alone is nothing. To say you have faith is an empty statement. Tell us what your faith is in. Don't say you believe, say what you believe.

Oh, I know sometimes what we call faith doesn't have an object. There's a kind of Mary Poppins sort of "I have confidence in confidence alone" positive thinking. Without an object of the confidence, it is empty. It is a sweet, sickly, sugary, sentimental approach, which accomplishes the same results in our spirit and character as sugar does to our bodies. It tastes good and it's pleasant, but once into our system it often causes depression and results in fat, not muscle.

A popular song of some years back illustrates this kind of empty faith. Now I know at this point my wife is probably very nervous. Years ago, in another church, I sang this song to illustrate this point. Watching and listening to Guy Hovis, it looks so easy to sing. Fortunately for you, I have tried it and have already learned it is not easy. I'll not sing the song for two reasons. One, it has notes that are out of my range, and two, I can't sing the notes in my range. But the song "I Believe," when sung well, goes like this: "I believe for every drop of rain that falls a flower grows. I believe that somewhere in the darkest night a candle glows. Every time I hear a newborn baby cry or touch a leaf or see the sky, then I know why I believe."

That kind of faith doesn't cut it because it is not anchored firmly to the one who made the sky and the trees, who Himself is the only light in the darkness and gives light to us all.

All who come to God must believe that He is and that He is a rewarder of those who diligently seek Him (Hebrews 11:6).

There is born in all of us an awareness of God. The fact that all people discuss the existence of God and argue about it is the best evidence that this simple natural awareness is there. So much discussion on the part of those who stress this simple, natural awareness of God is the best support of Romans 1:20, which tells us God makes us aware of Him.

Some say that you must choose between faith and reason, but it is not so. You must choose between two faiths, human faith and divine faith. Human faith seeks to deny the natural awareness of God in you and tries to make you afraid of it and ashamed of it. You are asked to believe in a limited, external faith in human society with all its assumptions and prejudices. It is based on fear of being left out, of being ridiculed in your need to belong.

Divine faith does not draw its light from human reason and intelligence. It is instead a spiritual light for the intellect. It is not contradictory of reason, but it transcends reason in a way that is reasonable. It answers questions about who you are, about why you can love, about your innate desire to do right, and about many other things that human faith cannot answer. It transcends reason in a way that is reasonable.

Divine faith therefore has the right object and is intelligent. Faith is a spiritual light for the intellect coming from beyond the sphere of our own intelligence. Anselm said, "I believe in order to understand." Intelligent faith struggles with questions.

When Abram asked how He was going to make a hundred-year-old man the father of a nation with a seventy-five-year-old wife who was not now and in fact never had been able to have a child, God said simply, "Look at the stars." The God who can make more stars than you can count can do this thing too. And Abram believed Him.

Faith begins with God. It is the essence of faith that we find life's answers outside ourselves. We have faith in what we do not see, and in the transcendent and invisible God. It is faith that gives us life in the spirit and in Christ. The just live by faith, the apostle testifies, "The life which I now live in the flesh I live by faith in Jesus Christ."

This brings us to the realization that we can bring a kind of human faith into church. We can be a member of the church and be a Christian in name only. We can belong to the church, not as a part of the Body of Christ, but as a member of an institution and an occasional and regular part of a religious audience.

We can conform generally to accepted norms of Christian behavior, not out of love for God, but in order to live up to minimal standards of conduct that guarantee acceptance by the group. Christ made clear the direct opposition between faith and mere human respect: "How can you believe if you accept praise from one another, yet make no effort to obtain the praise that comes from the only God?" (John 5:44).

Abram believed God and it was credited to him as righteousness. It was credited to him as righteousness. He was not righteous. We have already seen that. Abram did some things both dumb and bad, just like you and me. But because he believed, it was credited to him as righteousness. This is the first biblical statement of the truth clearly stated in Ephesians 2:8–9: "For it is by grace you have been saved, through faith... it is the gift of God—not by works, so that no one can boast."

Your salvation and mine comes not from our own mind, not from our working for it, but from the God of love and grace. "Abram believed God and it was credited to him as righteousness." All who come to God must believe that He is and that He is a rewarder of those who diligently seek Him. Romans 4:21 declares that Abram was fully persuaded that God was able to do what He had promised.

That is divine faith. That is the faith which leads to life's highest rewards. How can you know that you have the divine faith? Well, of course, the answer is in your own heart and will. But there are two repeated evidences of saving faith, two questions you can ask yourself that will reveal your faith.

First, how well do you obey? Do you try to learn from God's Word what He expects of you and then do it? In Genesis 15:8, Abram asked God, "How can I know that what you've said is true?" God did not answer his question. Instead He commanded Abram to bring an offering to Him and worship Him. Abram did just as He was told and learned that the assurance of faith comes through obedience. Hebrews 11:8 says: "By faith Abram, when called... obeyed and went, even though he did not know where he was going." Do you believe? How well do you obey?

Second, how much do you pray? Prayer is the heart of our faith. Jesus said, "I want my Father's house to be known as a house of prayer." We come into a saving relationship with God through a prayer of faith. We find both the will and the strength to do it through prayer.

You want to be saved? Come to God and pray: "O Lord, you're right about sin; it is not good. It is destructive. Therefore, I turn from my sin and I am asking Christ to come into my life and be my Savior and Lord."

You want to know wisdom, to know what to do? James 1:5: "If any of you lacks wisdom, he should ask God...and it will be given to him." But ask in faith. You want to live in strength and joy of God's presence and power. Hear Jesus say, "If you human fathers know how to give good gifts to your children when they ask for them, don't you know my Father will grant you His Holy Spirit if you will ask for Him!"

Wouldn't it be great, if in telling your life story, some child or grandchild, spouse or friend would add this editorial comment? "He (or she) believed God and received life's highest reward."

Chapter 17

The Way to Heaven

Romans 3:21–24

In preaching class, they told us about a minister years ago who wrote for himself not only sermon notes, but also suggestions in the margins about how to deliver the sermons, such as "speak slowly and convincingly here," "speak with enthusiasm," or "speak fast, your logic is weak."

Well, I often speak fast when I preach, and I'm not apologizing for a weakness of logic or difficulty in expressing truth. Don't all of us have trouble expressing logically and clearly the real, big things in life? Little things can be expressed clearly and logically but not the big things—things like beauty, love, devotion, and God.

If we could make God logical and reduce Him to our thinking, He wouldn't be the great God that He is, or we would be much greater than we are. The fact is God is not overly interested, I think, in our logic, at least not human logic. One day, we will probably learn we are really terribly illogical, but He is interested in love.

Romans 1 tells us there is no logical way of getting to heaven. You have heard people say, "All roads lead to heaven. Just believe what you believe." These verses in Holy Writ tell us that the roads we think lead to heaven do not get us there.

Proverbs 14:12 tells us, "There is a way that seems right to a man, but in the end it leads to death." Well, you've heard those ways: (1) "I'll do the best I can." (2) "I'll follow my conscience and trust my heart." (3) "I'll keep some rules, join the church, and be religious." Those ideas of getting to heaven are a summary of human and biblical history.

In the Garden of Eden, people were innocent. God gave them just one rule, and they failed. For the next period of history, people followed their consciences. They did what they thought was right. They lived their own lives, and what did they become? Genesis 6:5 says, "The LORD saw how great man's wickedness on the earth had become, and that every inclination of the thoughts of his heart was only evil all the time."

Then people said, "Well, we do need some ethical and moral laws. Just give us the guidelines, Lord, and we will live well and earn our way to heaven." God gave them the law, and once again, there was failure. Romans 3:9–19 could be headed, as in my Bible, "No One Is Righteous." God does not see us as students needing to be enlightened. He does not see us as patients needing to be healed. He sees us as a judge who looks at the accused.

The charge is "for all have sinned and fall short of the glory of God." All are under the dominion of sin. All are deficient and fall short of the standards of righteousness. The evidence is presented. The way people act, the wars, the things around us, the things people do or think, their words or works, prove them guilty.

The verdict is no one is righteous. No one is worthy. So we dreadfully await the logical sentence. There is nothing else logically left. We wait for the dreaded "therefore." (1) "All are guilty, therefore. . . ." (2) "There is none that doeth good, not even one, therefore. . . ."

But the logical "therefore" does not come. It is the illogical "but now" we read. "But now I'm showing you the way to heaven, a way for you to be righteous and perfect in God's sight." It's illogical. It's like being in court. The evidence has been overwhelmingly presented and proven our guilt. The verdict is clear. You stand before the judge, and he says, "You're guilty. Case dismissed."

It is not that the moral and ethical laws have been repealed. They have not. It is just that we can't be perfect, and God gives us His perfection through Jesus Christ. You see, it's not about logic; it's about love. It's not about our being loved because we are lovely or valuable. It's about our being valuable because we are loved.

Quite frankly, I find very little in me to give me self-worth and value. I find my value and self-worth in the fact that I am loved by some wonderful people and especially that I am loved by God. There is a logical kind of love in which lovely people are loved because they are lovely. There is the illogical, wonderful love of God in which we know we are valuable only because we are loved.

Rosemary was three when Rag Doll came into her life. Her family had flown across an ocean to move to a new country. A kind woman with the group to meet them knew that a three-year-old would be coming, and she prepared a gift for the occasion. She made a simple rag doll. Rosemary was totally jet-lagged and somewhat anxious. Tears sort of sat there in the corners of her eyes, and when given the rag doll, she was too tired to say, "Thank you." But she clutched the rag doll to her face to cover her tears.

That night, she still had the tears, and she still clutched Rag Doll. Then the tears were gone, and for many, many years, she was very, very close to Rag Doll. She always had her with her. Rosemary had a lot of playthings that were more costly and of more intrinsic value than Rag Doll, but nothing was more valuable to her.

In time, a problem arose concerning Rag Doll. She became more ragged and less doll. Rag Doll became dirty and stained. If you tried to get the dirt and stain out, you made her more ragged still. There was only one logical decision. Trash Rag Doll. But if you knew Rosemary, that was not a choice. If you loved Rosemary, you loved Rag Doll.

You and I are God's rag dolls—ragged, dirty, and stained. The logical thing is to trash us, but that's not even thinkable to Him.

If you love God, you love His rag dolls. Isn't that what the Bible says in 1 John? You can't love God and hate your brother. The Lord says, "Love Me; love my rag doll."

So it is not "You're guilty, therefore. . . ." It is "You are undeniably guilty, but you are unconditionally loved." A "righteousness from God has been made known." He has made a way to be right with Him, to have His peace, to go to heaven. This way God has made does not depend on our merit or our efforts. In Romans 3:21, it is "a righteousness from God apart from law." It simply means that Jesus came down here and kept the law for you and me. The way God has made is based on His grace.

Romans 3:24 says, "and are justified freely by his grace through the redemption that came by Christ Jesus." We are justified. That means we become "not guilty." We are justified freely. "Freely" means without a cause. We can do nothing to cause our justification. It is not my own work. It is by His grace.

You remember Ephesians 2:8–9, "For it is by grace you have been saved, through faith—and this not from yourselves, it is the gift of God—not by works, so that no one can boast." It is the gift of God, not of works.

Someone dreamed of dying and appearing at the gates of heaven. The gatekeeper said, "It takes two hundred points to get into heaven. Review your life, and I will award the appropriate points."

The man said, "Well, I'm sure I'll make it. I've been an active member of the church for more than sixty-two years, and I've given a great deal of money to Christian causes."

The gatekeeper said, "That's worth one point."

"Well," the man said, "I've been a faithful husband, an honest businessman, and involved in many community projects."

The gatekeeper said, "That will be one point."

The man's "flabber" was "gasted." He said, almost in a panic, "If the judging is that difficult, then the grace of God is my only hope."

Then the gatekeeper gave him one hundred ninety-eight points.

The fact is all two hundred points come only by the grace of God. We are justified freely by His grace through the redemption that comes by Jesus Christ. Jesus paid it all. We receive this right standing with God through faith in Jesus Christ.

The righteousness from God comes by faith in Jesus Christ to all who believe. We are not saved by faith; we are saved by grace, and our salvation comes through faith in the Lord Jesus Christ.

Here is a vital question. What does it mean to believe in Jesus Christ? What is faith? Is it just knowledge of truth? It is that, but it is more. It is also acceptance of truth. But it is more. Faith is knowledge and acceptance of truth and trust and surrender to truth.

Suppose I asked you, "Do you believe in George Washington? Do you have faith in George Washington?"

Well, you know there was George Washington, and you accept the fact that George Washington was our first president and many other things you've been taught. But you don't believe in or have faith in George Washington unless you place your trust in him and give your life to him to deliver you.

You may say, "I know about Jesus Christ. I accept the truth about Jesus Christ. He is the Son of God. He died on the cross. He was resurrected from the grave." But you believe in Him, your faith is in Him, only when you give Him your life to deliver you.

Chapter 18

God's Kindness

2 Samuel 9:1–7

Have you ever loved someone, reached out to them, given them everything you had, cared about them deeply, and then had that love abused and had them walk away? If so, then you know something that God knows.

Are you willing, if that one you loved and who abused your love were to come back, are you willing that without any proof that things would be different, without anything other than just asking to be received, you love them so much that you would welcome them again? If that is so, then there is another way you're somewhat like God.

In these recent weeks as we've talked about the difference between the Allah of Islam, the teachings of Buddha, the Hindu teachings, the god of Jehovah's Witnesses and Mormons, we've said the difference is that our religion is not a religion of works. It is by His wonderful, free, undeserved, unmerited grace that God has saved us. We cannot earn it. We cannot buy it. We cannot learn it and pass tests and get it. We cannot take it with the strength of our character. It is God's grace, His grace.

And I've gotten some letters. I had a pastor friend, when I was his assistant pastor in our very first church, who received an anonymous letter one day that just had one word written in large letters on the page. The word was "fool." He said: "You know, I've gotten a lot of letters where people wrote the letter and didn't sign their name. But this is the first time I've ever gotten a letter where someone signed their name and didn't write the letter."

I've gotten a lot of anonymous mail lately and interestingly enough, most of it is very, very kind and very, very nice. But there have been a couple of letters, one signed and one unsigned, which said, "You're making it look as though you can sin and do anything you want to do and still be a Christian. You're giving people a license to do anything they want to do and live any way they want to live and God will still love them and save them." They said: "People are going to quit coming to church. They're going to quit giving. The budget will go down the tube. People are not going to support God's work unless you keep them a little bit frightened about their salvation." And yet God seems to risk like that.

In Romans 6, after the apostle Paul has been saying to people: "When you come to God, you come to a God of grace who loves you and He gives you your salvation. It's a free gift. It is outside the works of the law." And then in Chapter 6, he begins to say, "But some of you are going to say, 'Why don't we sin all the more so that grace can abound? Let's really let this grace work. Let's just keep sinning.'"

And a dearly beloved seminary professor once said: "If you are preaching the gospel of Jesus Christ, you are going to be accused, like Paul was, of preaching something that is impractical, of preaching something that people cannot accept. The idea that God loves us without our earning it, the idea that God saves us without our deserving it, is something that people don't want to believe. It is hard for people to believe that God is not like them. It's hard for people to believe that they are not just a little reproduction of God to the extent that, whatever they feel, God feels; whatever they think, God thinks. But your biggest job as a preacher of the gospel of Jesus Christ is to convince people that God is not like them, that He is a God of grace, a God of love. He is the God of unconditional love."

There are three things we can do when we're sinned against, the same three things God could do when He is sinned against. One is vengeance. Another is justice. And the other is grace.

If someone were to murder your child, brutally, cruelly, murder and take the life of your beloved child, you have these three options. You could say, "I will get vengeance. I will make sure that I will get my revenge. This person killed my child. I'll kill them."

Or you could say, "I'll let the system take care of him. There will be a trial and there'll be a guilty verdict and there will be an execution. That's justice."

But if you were to say, "I will forgive the one who murdered my child: I will love the one who murdered my child, in fact, I will invite that one to come into my home and be my child and take the place of the child that they murdered." My friend, that would be great. And that's why God is so different than we are.

In this past week, I've been looking at that story in 2 Samuel 7 where David did that interesting thing. With no reason other than the kindness of his heart, with no prompting other than the love for the father of Mephibosheth who was David's best friend, David finds a young man who is socially, economically, and even physically unacceptable to the people around him. He brings him into his home and he makes him his son and he showers him with more gifts and more love and more acceptance than you could imagine. He does it all saying, "I'm showing God's kindness." Maybe this is what the Scripture has in mind when God says: "David is a man after my own heart." What David did is like what God does.

But then we read a few chapters later in 2 Samuel 16 that this young man who had been brought out of poverty and denial and brought into the most beautiful situation ever, that this young man, when the opportunity presented itself, responded by trying to take the kingdom away from the one who had been so good to him.

I thought: What an abusing of love! What a tragic and terrible abusing of love!

Then I realized that, to one degree or another, that's my story and yours. We've all abused the love of God. We've all taken advantage of the kind of love that God gives to us. Just like the people who've written me this week said, "People will abuse God's love if you tell them He loves them so much He forgives them by grace."

Yet the whole Word, the Bible from beginning to end, is the story of God's love being abused. Sometimes people say to me: "Well, the New Testament is about grace but the Old Testament is about law." That's not true. Grace drips from every page of the Old Testament. As you read the working of God with His people, those pages are filled with God's grace. The very first story in Eden shows us Adam and Eve. They have been given life and livelihood and love and paradise and they sin against that. They are literally saying in their sin, "God, we don't want you. We don't need you. We will be god of our lives. We will go our own way. We will do our thing."

And how did God respond to that? Not by sending an executioner, not by sending judge and jury, but He came down Himself to see how much He could just preserve, how much He could salvage of these rebellious children whom He loved so much even though they didn't love Him.

You remember the story of Jonah. I think that's one of the most fascinating stories I've ever read anywhere. It's about a reluctant missionary who didn't like the people God told him to preach to. He tried to run from God's will. He would not go to Nineveh, yet he was forced to be there. When he was there, he delivered the message without emotion, without passion, probably without even enthusiasm. He told the people of Nineveh: "God said you are going to be destroyed because the sin you have committed is now tumbling in on you; and that destruction is coming." He did not say: "God said, 'Repent.'" He did not say anything except: "God told you that you are going to be destroyed." And they thought themselves: "Maybe if we repent, maybe if we turn from sin and turn to God, He will be gracious to us." Jonah, who had not one whit of love for them, who had told them their story with no love in his heart, went out on the side of a hill east of town so he could get a good view of the destruction. Then he realized God wasn't going to destroy them, and it made him angry. It made him so angry, we read in the fourth chapter of Jonah, that Jonah prayed to the Lord: "Oh, Lord, is this not what I said when I was still at home? That's why I was so quick to go to Tarshish instead of coming here. I knew that you are a gracious and compassionate God, slow to anger and abounding in love, a God who relents from sending calamity."

"And now, Lord," he said, "I'm so mad I could die." The last lines of Jonah say this. These are the words of God: "But Nineveh has more than 120,000 people who cannot tell their right hand from their left, and many cattle as well, should I not be concerned about that great city?"

God is not like us. He loves those who don't love Him. He cares for those who sin against Him. God is a God of great grace and wants to love all who will come to Him, and He does love them and He does care. God is not like us.

I talked to a pastor friend just a few days ago. He told me about a young lady who came to see him. She was a young wife and mother. Her adultery had wrought havoc in their home. And she sobbed out and cried and just bawled and talked and told her sordid story of all the things she had done. Every time she took a breath, the pastor looked at her and smiled and called her name and said: "God loves you." Then she would start talking again and when she had to take a breath, the pastor would smile and say: "God loves you." And when this happened the third time, she retorted angrily: "Don't tell me God loves me. I'm a parent. I know how I feel when my kids mess up. I know how I feel about them when they do these things. Don't tell me God loves me." And he said: "Honey, God isn't like you. God isn't like you." And that's the story we need to learn. God isn't like us.

You remember that strange and wonderful story of Hosea, contemporary of Jeremiah. While Jeremiah was getting into very deep trouble by telling the truth in the capitol of the nation, Hosea was out preaching in little towns and villages. He was what they called a minor prophet. He was young. One day he saw a young lady. She was beautiful, vivacious, with a wonderful personality. He was attracted to her. He said: "Who is that?" His friends said: "Well, her name is Gomer but you don't want to know her. She's not like us. She has a very lustful background. In fact, the religion she worshiped in her father's house is based upon love. You don't want to know her."

But he did want to know her. He cultivated the friendship and their friendship became love and soon they were married. Here this young man Hosea was leaving home and going out and preaching in his circuit, writing prophecy, and when he would come back home, he would come back to this wonderful wife and their first years were good. A son was born, and then a daughter.

About this time, Hosea's friends began to tell him things. He said: "No, I don't believe that. Gomer wouldn't be doing that. I know she misses her former life and she misses the parties and she misses all the luxuries she had in her father's home, but she wouldn't do that. She wouldn't do that."

When the third child, the second son, was born, God, who in those days did that, told Hosea, "You name this child Lo-ammi," which translated means "not one of us." And the truth hit Hosea. When confronted, Gomer denied it at first and said, "No it's not so. This hasn't happened." Finally, as he persisted, her face hardened and her eyes narrowed and she said, "All right, it's true. I've had not just one lover, but I've had many lovers. What are you going to do about it?" She walked out the door, slammed it, and left him with the children.

One night, says the Word, Hosea was sitting in his home, maybe with the child of her unfaithfulness in his lap, and God said, "Hosea, you've been telling people that their unfaithfulness to me breaks my heart, haven't you?"

Hosea said, "Yes, Lord, I have."

God said, "But now you know, don't you, Hosea?"

And Hosea said, "Yes, Lord, I know."

As Hosea sat there and thought about Gomer and wondered what she was doing, the thoughts that came to his mind were so painful he tried hard to think of something else. We see this man grieving, his love abused, and the love of his life having turned away from him. We're seeing something that we need to see clearly, for when we sin, we sin against love. When you sin, you sin against love, not against laws, not against rules. When you sin, you sin against love.

God said, "Hosea, you've been telling those people that their unfaithfulness hurts me. And now you know, don't you?"

Hosea said, "Yes, Lord, I know."

God said, "But you still love her, don't you?"

Hosea said, "Yes, Lord, I do."

"And you want her back, don't you?"

"Yes, I do."

God said, "Hosea, in the morning Gomer is going to be auctioned off as a slave at the slave market. I want you to go get all your life savings—all fifteen pieces of silver. I want you to go to the barn and get all that's left of the barley harvest for this year, and in the morning you go and you buy Gomer back."

Early the next morning, Hosea was seen walking briskly down the street. Jangling in the purse at his side were fifteen silver coins. On his back was a little sack with a homer and a half of barley, all that was left of the barley harvest. He had taken everything he had to go to the slave auction. When he got there he was shocked by what he saw. He had never been to that place before. But the thing that shocked him the most was seeing Gomer. She was already on the auction block. Her beautiful, bright, shiny hair was now dull and matted because it was so dirty. Rags hung around her dirty body. And that face, which at one time was perfect, was marked and lined with sin. Here's another picture of sin that seems so trivial when it began, but becomes a tragedy. Sin is always a tragedy.

Hosea went to the auctioneer and laid fifteen pieces of silver on the table and the homer and a half of barley and said: "Is it enough? Is it enough to buy Gomer? Is it enough?" It was enough, because no one else wanted her now. It was enough. He took her by the hand and began to walk her back to their home. She used to walk so proudly by his side, flaunting the beauty that God had given her. But now she walked more slowly and stooped. They turned that familiar corner down the road, to the lane where they lived, and she walked the place that she had walked so many times before. When he opened the gate for her and then opened the door for her, she began to realize that Hosea was taking her not just back into his home, but into his heart. Then I think some of Gomer's beauty began to return to her.

In this story God is saying to you and me, "Just as that man took everything he had, out of the love for the one who had rejected and abused his love totally, just as he took everything he had to buy her back because he loved her, I've given everything I have. I love you like that," says God, "I've given myself. I've given my Son. I've given my life. I've given my all because I want you back."

"For God so loved the world that He gave His only begotten Son that whoever believes in Him will not perish but have everlasting life." Whoever, you-ever, believes in Him will not perish but have everlasting life.

Maybe you're a Christian and you say: "Well, Lord, one day I pledged my love for you and I abused that love and I walked away from it. I've messed up." God says, "I want you back. I want you back because I love you. I love you."

Maybe you say, "I'm thinking about becoming a Christian and

yet I can't see how you would forgive me. I wouldn't forgive me if I were you." God says, "You're not me. I'm not like you. I am the God who loves and wants to forgive."

You may say, "But I don't feel like I could live up to it." I have a brother. For more than thirty-five years, I witnessed to him and every time he said, "I'm not ready yet because I don't think I could live up to it." God says, "That's true. You can't live up to it. You're never going to be able to live up to it. That's alright because I love you and I want to give you salvation."

This is the grace of God who loves you so much He wants you to live forever. You can't be good enough. You can't give enough. You can't go enough. You can't do enough. All you can do is to say, "Lord, just as I am, without one plea, but that thy blood was shed for me; O Lamb of God, I come, I come."

For by grace you have been saved through faith. It is the gift of God, not of works, lest anyone should boast.

Chapter 19

Hope for the Broken Family

Luke 6:27–36

A few years ago a seminary professor, not our brand, worked up a sermon about love. Everywhere he went, he preached his sermon about love. In a church one day, a couple heard that sermon and asked him, "Would you talk to our daughter? She's nineteen, an alcoholic, and out of control." It was arranged. The professor said, "When I first saw her I thought, 'Young lady, if you're feeling all right, would you please tell your face?'" She was totally unhappy with a very large attitude. They met several times. He listened to her, and the more he listened the more assured he was that she was the most self-centered person he had ever met, totally unloving and uncaring. One day he decided to confront her with her self-centered attitude. "You know what you need? You need a Copernican Revolution. You need to learn that the world doesn't revolve around you. You live in a world where the population is one." The girl stomped out of his office.

A month later a psychiatrist came to lecture at the seminary. After the meeting the professor asked the psychiatrist, "How do you get people to love, not to be self-centered?" "Why do you ask that question?" The professor told about the girl.

"I don't think you can get people to love," said the psychiatrist. "It's a decision of the will and a commitment people must decide to and commit themselves to it. But if you really wanted to help that young lady learn to love, you did it exactly wrong."

"How's that?"

"Did you ever have a toothache?"

"Well, yes."

"What did you think about when you had a toothache?"

"Well, I thought about me."

"Who else?"

"A dentist."

"That's right. When you're hurting, you can't think about

anyone else except yourself and someone you think might can help you get rid of the pain. That girl was hurting. When she came to you, you were nice and she said to herself, 'Maybe this is the one who can relieve my pain, maybe this is my dentist.' So she came out from behind the mask and revealed herself to you. She is selfish because she is hurting so much. Someone has given her such a bad image of herself that she reflects that image. They told her she is selfish and uncaring and worthless and she's just playing the role they gave her. She doesn't go to church like her parents want her to, not because she doesn't want to but because she thinks if she goes, God may say to her, 'What are you doing here, you slut!' Because that's what her father says to her. When she opened herself to you, you told her that her father was right. You said you didn't like her either."

"I didn't say that."

"Oh, you didn't? You said 'You need a Copernican Revolution; your world is just revolving around you; you live in a world with a population of one.' You didn't have to say I don't like you."

The world has a lot of people who are hurting. They are hurting so much all they can think of is themselves and how much they hurt. It's more than a toothache. A toothache does not cause people to take their lives. After alcohol and drug abuse, which they hope will deaden the hurt, the number one cause of death among young people is suicide. They're hurting and they're looking for some one to take away the hurt.

The loveless and uncaring people are the ones who desperately need our love. Our Lord Christ, who is the best lover of the unlovable, the best acceptor of the unacceptable, the best forgiver of the unforgivable, has gathered His people together and said, "I want you to change your world. I want you to represent me and be my ambassadors. I love this world. I will die for it, and I want you to do this:" (Luke 6:27–36)

27. *Love your enemies, do good to those who hate you,*
28. *bless those who curse you, pray for those who mistreat you.*
29. *If someone strikes you on one cheek, turn to him the other also.*
    If someone takes your cloak, do not stop him from taking your

tunic.

30. *Give to everyone who asks you, and if anyone takes what belongs to you, do not demand it back.*
31. *Do to others as you would have them do to you.*
32. *If you love those who love you, what credit is that to you? Even 'sinners' love those who love them.*
33. *And if you do good to those who are good to you, what credit is that to you? Even 'sinners' do that.*
34. *And if you lend to those from whom you expect repayment, what credit is that to you? Even 'sinners' lend to 'sinners,' expecting to be repaid in full.*
35. *But love your enemies, do good to them, and lend to them without expecting to get anything back. Then your reward will be great, and you will be sons of the Most High, because he is kind to the ungrateful and wicked.*
36. *Be merciful, just as your Father is merciful.*

He began by saying, "But I tell you who hear me." These demanding, challenging words are for those who hear Him. Who are you listening to? What voice? What authority directs your lifestyle? For those who hear Him, the Word is love. He says, "If you're going to love me you must learn how to love."

If we're going to learn how to love, we must understand what love is. You remember the fellow who took a long look across the gap and said:

Remember when hippy meant big in the hips?
And a trip involved cars, planes, and ships?
And pot was a vessel for cooking things in?
And hooked is what grandmother's rug might have been?
When neat meant well organized, tidy, and clean?
And grass was a ground cover, normally green?
When lights and not people were turned on and off?
And the pill could be what you took for a cough?
When fuzz was a substance fluffy like lint?
And bread came from bakeries, not from a mint?
When square meant a 90-degree angle form?

And cool was a temperature, not quite warm?
When roll was a bun, and rock was a stone?
And hang up is what you'd do with a phone?
When chicken meant poultry and bag meant a sack?
And junk, trashy castoffs and old bric-a-brac?
When swinger was someone who swung in a swing?
And pad was a soft sort of cushiony thing?
When dig meant to shovel and spade in the dirt?
Put on was what you'd do with a shirt?
Words once so sensible, sober, and serious
Are making the freak scene like psycho-delirious.
It's groovy man, but English, it's not.
Methinks the language has gone straight to pot!

The old saw, "I know you believe you understood what you think I said, but you don't realize that what you heard is not what I meant" probably can apply most of all to our confusion about the meaning of love.

Love is a verb. Love is an action. Some people treat it like a noun or an adjective. "I have not found love." "I am in love." "I'm not in love." When Jesus speaks of love, it is action. It is something you do. When, in God's Word, love is a noun, it is a synonym for God, who is love in action.

The world's love is reactive. Verses 32 and following declare what is readily seen. It is our natural bent to love those who love us, to do good to those who do good to us. When Jesus said, "If you love those who love you, what credit is that to you?" the word credit is the word *charis*. It is also translated in the Bible as "gift," as in the gift of the Spirit. It's also translated as "grace." If you only love those who love you, if you only do good to those who do good to you, where is the grace? Where is the evidence of God's Spirit in that?

The world's love is reactive. "Love me, and I'll love you. Do good to me, and I'll do good to you. Hate me, and I'll hate you. Slander me, and I'll slander you. Curse me, and I'll curse you. Slap me on the jaw, and I'll hit you in the stomach." It's blow for blow, tit for tat, action and reaction.

Reaction means you're not in control. You're letting others

decide how you will feel and what you will do. Jesus said, "If you're going to follow Me and represent Me, you must love like Me." God's love is active. It is not: "Do unto others as they have done to you," but "Do unto others as you would have them do to you."

A young woman grew up in a home where her stepfather sexually molested her for a number of years. When she married, she could not relate to her husband. She needed very much to be touched and hugged and yet, because she transferred her hatred for her stepfather toward all men, including her husband, she could not let her husband touch her. There was in her too much bitterness and shame.

She came to her pastor with the problem and he read to her Luke 6:27–28, and asked her what the Bible says you should do for your enemies. She said, "Love them, do good to those who hate you, pray for those who abuse you." He said, "That's what you must do to your stepfather if you're to be free from your bitterness." Every fiber in her being revolted against such advice. "How can I love him, do good to him, pray for him, and bless him after all the terrible things he did to me?" Yet she decided to apply the Scriptures. The Scripture says "Do good to your enemies," so she cooked him a birthday cake when his birthday came along. It says, "Bless those who curse you." She decided that she would stop speaking evil against him and to start speaking well. When she began to think about him, there were many good things she discovered. In many ways he was a good father. "Pray for those who abuse you" said the Scriptures. She decided to pray three times a day for him. And she decided to forgive him. Forgiveness is not a feeling; forgiveness is an action. She, by the grace of God, chose to forgive her stepfather. A few weeks later she said she saw him walking across the parking lot with an armful of groceries at the supermarket and she said, "Were it not for the previous relationship, I could have put my arms around him. I have forgiven him. Now I am free to love my husband."

If there is any hope for this world, there must be people who love unconditionally, accepting and loving the people who are hurting so much that they are bitter and angry and cannot love back. Those people ought to be God's people. There ought to be a place for hurting people to come and know they will be loved and accepted when to the rest of the world they are unlovely and unacceptable. That place ought to be the church of the Lord Jesus Christ.

But you say, "Preacher, I can't love like that." Of course you can't. Only God can love like that, but if you have God in you, if you've been born again, the Scripture declares that "the love of God is shed abroad in our hearts." Love is the gift of the spirit, the primary gift of the spirit. Love is the fruit of the spirit. "For the fruit of the spirit is love, joy, peace." Then your reward will be great and you'll be sons, children of the Most High.

Would you come to Him and be loved? Then you'll be free to love Him, to love others, and even love yourself—and it all begins in Jesus Christ.

Chapter 20

You Can Make a Difference

Ephesians 4:29–32; Acts 4:20

How many of you want a fulfilled life? You want life to be meaningful and not meaningless. Did you ever say, "I am bored" or "Let's get out of here and go somewhere that's fun"? Have you believed the world's lie that self-gratification is the way of life?

Now you have many of the goods of life but no life, almost everything to live with and nothing to live for. You're ready to say, "I want my life to mean something. I want to make a difference in this world. But I'm not flashy or dominant or brilliant."

Listen closely to our Lord Christ. From the Sermon on the Mount found in Matthew 5:13–16, "You are the light of the world." "You are the salt of the earth." Jesus said you are "salt" and "light." He didn't say you have to be flashy, brilliant, dominant. In fact, He doesn't ask you to be anything. He tells you what you are if you are a Christian. You are salt and light. What interesting metaphors: salt and light.

There are some common denominators. Both are subtle, almost unnoticed, yet make a vast difference. How many times do you walk into a room and say, "Wow! Look at the light." Now sometimes we notice the light fixtures. Yet nothing could happen after seven o'clock without the light. How often do you eat a steak or fish or a vegetable and say, "What great salt!" Yet without the salt the food is often tasteless, like life.

How can you make a difference? God's Word tells you, and what a super thing God's Word shows you! For in the New Testament there lived a man who made more difference in his world, who affected the first century more than any other person outside our Lord Christ. He did it not by promoting Himself, but just the opposite. He changed his world by pointing away from himself. He exercised no special gifts. He did no sensational spiritual tricks. We have no text of a sermon he preached nor a song he wrote nor an organization he founded, yet he impacted his world for Christ more than any other mortal of his day. In his ministry, he encouraged. He put people up instead of down. He never said, "You blew it." He constantly said, "You can do it!"

Later on we will learn from this splendid person how we too can change our world. Right now, let's look at his life and see an example of what God had in mind when He said, "Now I'll make me a man."

In Acts 4:36 we read the first mention of him. Everyone thinks his name was Barnabas but it wasn't. His name was Joseph. He was a member of the Jewish tribe of Levi. He was from Cyprus. The apostles called him Barnabas and the nickname caught on. *Bar* means "son of" and the rest of the name means "consolation" or "encouragement." If we translated the name Barnabas into our language, it might mean "Mr. Encourager."

In this Scripture we are told that Mr. Encourager sold some land he owned and made the proceeds of this sale a gift to our Lord through the church where he was a member in Jerusalem.

As the exciting history of the working of Christ through His people continues, we find Barnabas's name coming up again in chapter 9 of the book of Acts. An unbelievable thing had happened. Saul of Tarsus, the brilliant, feisty fighter of followers of Christ, committed to eradicating the name of our Lord Christ from the earth, met Christ and became a believer. Immediately he began to share his newfound faith in Damascus. This so angered his former allies that they sought to kill him. They guarded every gate to the town, determined not to let him escape and do damage elsewhere. Enterprising Christians created an elevator for him. With a rope and a big basket, they lowered him from the wall of the city, and Saul of Tarsus came back to Jerusalem.

Beginning in verse 26, we read, "When he came to Jerusalem, he tried to join the disciples, but they were all afraid of him, not believing that he really was a disciple." They thought he was trying to trick them.

Verse 27 declares that Barnabas listened to him and believed him. Paul probably told Barnabas the same story he told and retold the rest of his life about the light and voice on the Damascus road, how Christ saved him and called him, of all people, a Pharisee, to spend the rest of his life telling Gentiles the Good News. Well, Barnabas believed him and brought him to the apostles. Because they trusted Barnabas, they accepted Saul. Saul went all over town telling people what had happened, winning every debate with the Grecian Jews. They decided, like the people in Damascus, they would silence him the same way they had thought they had silenced Christ, only this time less publicly. So they tried to kill him. Verse 30 says, "When the brothers learned of this, they took him down to Caesarea and sent him off to Tarsus." It could be as much as five years before we hear of Saul or Barnabas again.

Acts 11 reveals the exciting news of spiritual awakening in Antioch, a Gentile city. The church in Jerusalem sent Barnabas there to check it out. When he got there, he found evidence of the grace of God. Oh, how I pray that when people come to our church, they find evidence of the grace of God! So Barnabas was glad, and encouraged them to remain true to the Lord with all their hearts.

In verse 24, the Bible says of Barnabas, "He was a good man, full of the Holy Spirit and faith, and a great number of people were brought to the Lord."

Then Barnabas remembered something. About five years ago, Saul of Tarsus had told him that God had called him to minister to Gentiles, so Barnabas went to Tarsus. It doesn't look like a long way to go on the map, but remember that he either walked or rode a donkey. If you have ever ridden a donkey, you probably would rather walk. He found Saul, and just as he introduced him to the Jerusalem Christians, he introduced him to the Christians at Antioch. For a whole year, Barnabas and Saul discipled people in the church at Antioch. Those people so resembled Christ in their lifestyle that it was there that the people were first called Christians.

Well, a thing happened in that church which happens in all churches where Christ is Lord. They began to say to themselves, "If we needed Christ—and how we did!—then the people in the next towns need Him too, and the next town, and the next. In fact, the people in all the towns need Him." So missions were born in the hearts of the First Baptist Church of Antioch.

In Chapter 13 we read, "While they were worshiping the Lord and fasting, the Holy Spirit said, 'Set apart for me Barnabas and

Saul for the work to which I have called them.'" So after they had fasted and prayed, they laid their hands on them and sent them off. Off they went on the first missionary journey. What an exciting, adventurous and oft-times dangerous trip it was! You can read about it in Acts 13 and 14.

In the midst of the journey, an interesting thing happened. As all this started, there was no doubt that Saul was the leader. Acts 12:25 speaks of Barnabas and Saul coming back to Jerusalem. In Chapter 13:2, the Holy Spirit says, "Set apart for me Barnabas and Saul." In verse 7, it is Barnabas and Saul; and then in verse 9 we read of Saul, who is also called Paul. In verse 13, Paul and his companions; in verse 42, Paul and Barnabas; in verse 46, Paul and Barnabas.

Isn't that something? Barnabas apparently saw the gifts in Paul that led to him being the greatest missionary ever and author of half the New Testament, and instead of jealousy Barnabas felt joy. He didn't try to suppress Paul; he encouraged him, and willingly stepped into a secondary position so Paul could fulfill God's destiny for his life. He could have said, "Look, Saul or Paul, or whatever you call yourself, no one would know about you if it weren't for me. I stuck my neck out two miles to get you into the church in Jerusalem. I went all the way to Tarsus and back to bring you to Antioch, and now you are horning in on my territory." I don't think these thoughts occurred to either one of them; but I'm sure that it was Barnabas who made the decision. It was no longer Barnabas and Saul, but had become Saul and Barnabas.

When they got back to Antioch from that journey, it was still Paul and Barnabas. Chapter 15:35 states, "But Paul and Barnabas remained in Antioch, where they and many others taught and preached the Word of the Lord."

Sometime later, Paul said to Barnabas, "Let's go back and visit the churches we started and see how they're doing." Barnabas thought that was an excellent idea, and added a suggestion of his own. "Let's take John [also called Mark] with us."

Paul didn't like that idea at all. You see, John Mark had been with them on the first mission trip and had failed. He deserted them in Pamphylia and came back home. We are not told why. Maybe he got tired of putting up and taking down the tent. We don't know, but they disagreed so sharply that they parted ways over this. Paul took Silas and left, commended by the brothers to the grace of the Lord, says the Bible. The rest of their journey we read about in the following pages in Acts.

Does this mean they didn't commend Barnabas to the grace of the Lord? That they took Paul's side in this split? How that must have hurt! Says one line in the midst of all this, "Barnabas took Mark and sailed to Cypress." And I'm sure, aren't you, that every step of that journey, Barnabas let Mark do the witnessing and winning, and kept saying, "You can do it, Mark! Just because you failed once doesn't mean you are a failure. He always gives you another chance; and as many chances as you need. You can do it, Mark!"

And thus, John Mark believed again that God could use him; that somehow his life, though marred with failure, could make a difference.

Do you know that when the Holy Spirit of our Lord God commissioned the first writing of the life of Christ, it was written by John Mark? The Gospel of Mark is the first written account of the life of Christ.

Who is responsible for the greatest impact on Christian history in the first century? Is it the apostle Paul, the world's greatest missionary, martyr of our Lord Christ, and author of half the New Testament? Or is it the one without whom we would never have heard of Paul? Is it a greater thing in God's scheme of things to be author of the first written account of the life of Christ? Or to be the encourager who is responsible for bringing him back to the privilege of service? I believe Barnabas, Mr. Encourager, made a greater impact on his world in his day than any other, because without him we would never have had either the ministries of Paul or Mark. The spirit and ministry of Barnabas are the most effective in the Kingdom.

You can make a difference in your world if you will be an encourager.

Chapter 21

Don't Let the Mirror Lie to You

Joshua 14:9–14

Every sermon should have a subject. From the beginning, both the congregation and the preacher should know what the subject is. I want to talk to you today again about getting older.

In the Word of God, hear from Joshua 14 beginning in verse 9:

> So on that day Moses swore to me, "The land on which your feet have walked will be your inheritance and that of your children forever, because you have followed the LORD my God wholeheartedly.' Now then, just as the LORD promised, He has kept me alive for forty-five years since the time He said this Moses, while Israel moved about in the desert. So here I am today, eighty-five years old! I am still as strong today as the day Moses sent me out; I'm just as vigorous to go out to battle now as I was then. Now give me this hill country that the LORD promised me that day. You yourself heard then that the Anakites were there and their cities were large and fortified, but, the LORD helping me, I will drive them out just as He said." Then Joshua blessed Caleb son of Jephunneh and gave him Hebron as his inheritance. So Hebron has belonged to Caleb son of Jephunneh the Kenizzite ever since, because he followed the LORD, the God of Israel, wholeheartedly.

I have found in recent months some insightful reading about facing today's problems penned by that philosopher from Atlanta, Lewis Grizzard. Now I know these books aren't found in the recommended reading list of our Church Training division. He has written a book titled *They Tore My Heart Out and Stomped That Sucker Flat*, a bestseller and full of good insight into the experience of major surgery and its anxiety. In his book, *My Daddy Was a Pistol and I'm a Son of a Gun*, he humorously breaks your heart as he talks about being the son of an irresponsible and uncaring father. And he wrote a book about aging. It's titled *Elvis Is Dead and I Don't Feel So Good*

Myself. As a minister, I am tempted to write a sequel, *Billy Graham Is Old and I Don't Look So Young Myself.*

How I thank God for Billy Graham! While he has taken his calling very seriously, he has never taken himself too seriously. That's how a preacher or anyone else messes up. He has never been the Reverend Doctor William Franklin Graham. He's just been Billy, just as our Lord was never called Reverend Doctor Wholeness Angelic Divinity, Junior. When He was a human being showing us what a real human being is supposed to be like down here, everyone just called Him Jesus.

I saw an interview on television in which Billy Graham and another well-known religious personality were asked if anything bothered them. Now this other fellow talked in hyper-spiritual language. Does that bother you too? I don't like to hear people talk like that. It always makes me a little suspicious when I hear people talk like that. And this man told how spiritual and wonderful he was and how he walked so close to God there was simply nothing in the world that really bothered him. Then Billy Graham said: "Well, yes, I am bothered. I'm disturbed about getting old. I don't like it. I'm going to work through it. God will be with me in it, but right now it bothers me." Isn't that good?

Getting older bothered Moses. He said: "Lord, I'm eighty years old. I can't do this thing you've asked me to do." It bothered Abraham. He said: "Lord, I'm pushing a hundred. How can I experience the dreams you keep putting in my heart?" It's okay to be bothered, but it's wonderful to know that you can work through it.

Have you ever thought about how we know we're old? Who decides that? You know when it was decided that we should retire at sixty-five and that sixty-five was the mark of being old? It was one hundred and twenty-five years ago in Germany. They chose sixty-five as a marker of old age. Do you know what life expectancy was then? Forty-five years! People didn't worry about retirement. They didn't live that long. Do you know that now the average person's lifespan is seventy-five, and we're still believing that sixty-five is old! This has produced some myths about aging. People are, for the most part, wrong about aging.

What about health? Only eighteen percent of older people, according to a scientific study, believe they really have health problems. And that means that eighty-two percent of older people do not think they have health problems. Young people think that old people are all falling apart. But chronologically gifted people think they're fine. Young people think that all old people are poor and struggle to make ends meet. Well, some really do and that's very, very sad. But do you know there are more teenagers living at or below poverty level in our land than elderly people? Do you know there are six hundred thousand millionaires in the United States receiving Social Security? One-half of all the millionaires in America are over sixty-five. Sixty-five is not old any more. In fact, a leading expert says that we should take a new way of looking at aging. Forty to sixty should be seen as middle adulthood; sixty to eighty later adulthood; and you have to be at least eighty before you can call yourself old.

We think we're old long before we are. Why? Well, it's the terrible M & M twins—media and mirrors. In the media, they tell us that old is being wrinkled and gray. "When you see a wrinkle or a gray hair, buy our goop to smooth it out or rinse it away." There was a wonderful woman who walked into a drugstore and said: "Give me a jar of that Oil of Old Lady." While the media sell us on the idea of old, the mirror tells us we are old. History will one day name the mirror as one of life's largest detractors.

Have you ever had this experience? If you haven't, you will. You're feeling good. You're happy. You're full of vitality. You feel like you can do anything and life is good. And you walk by a mirror. There's an older person in there wearing your clothes. Because you see the wrinkles, because you see the gray, you think you're old, but you're not. Don't let the mirror lie to you! Old is not wrinkles and gray. Old is when you quit trying. Old is when you give up. Old is when you no longer dream of the things you'll do, the people you'll serve in the name of the God you love.

In the first church Jane and I served, there were seven deacons. The youngest was forty-seven; the oldest was eighty-eight. The Bible tells of an eighty-five-year-old young man. His name was Caleb. He's one of my heroes. "Forty-five years ago," he said, "I got this dream and I still have the dream. And I want that mountain." Caleb probably didn't have a mirror but if he did, he wouldn't let it lie to him.

Don't let the mirror lie to you. You are still you. Caleb said: "I am still the man I was forty-five years ago." Where is it written that you have to be old at eighty-five? You may quote to me the observation in Psalm 90:10 that people live three score and ten, or seventy years. But God intended us to live a hundred and twenty years. How do I know that? He said it in Genesis 6:3. He said, "My spirit will not contend with man forever, for he is mortal; his days will be one hundred and twenty years." Interestingly enough, the Rand Corporation and other scientific studies declare that the biological lifespan, the upper ceiling on the span of life that people are capable of living, is one hundred and twenty years.

When Congress cut Oliver Wendell Holmes's pension, he was ninety years old. Someone said: "Will you be able to live on that reduced income?" He said, "Yes, but I won't be able to save as much for my old age."

Rupert Richardson, the wonderful retired president of Hardin-Simmons University, was elected chairman of the deacons of the First Baptist Church of Abilene, Texas, when he was in his nineties. On his ninety-second birthday his friends gave him a party. In replying to their kindness, he said: "I read a very encouraging statistic today. I've learned that very few people die after the age of ninety-two."

Don't let the mirror lie to you. You are still you. You are still the person you were. Some people get older and never grow up; others grow up and never get older.

Don't let the mirror steal your dream. Caleb's dream after forty-five years was still alive. "Give me that mountain." Caleb is the kind of person who is my hero today. We all need heroes. When I was a teenager, my heroes were Joe DiMaggio and professional baseball players and athletes who were in their twenties and thirties. When I was a young man, my heroes were Billy Graham and other outstanding ministers in their thirties, forties, and fifties. And now my heroes are people like so many of you, who have grown up but never gotten older because you've kept your dream alive.

General Douglas MacArthur said: "People do not become old

by merely living a certain number of years. They become old when they desert their vision." Years wrinkle the skin, but giving up enthusiasm wrinkles the soul.

Do you know Anna Mary Robertson Moses? She was the mother of five children and the grandmother of eleven. At the age of eighty, she had her first one-woman art exhibit. She called it "What a Farm Wife Painted." The title, like her art, was straightforward and simple, but there was a power to her simplicity that captured those who observed. So for the next twenty-one years she continued to paint. We know her today as Grandma Moses.

Albert Schweitzer, at seventy-seven, won the Nobel Peace Prize and used the award to refinance an ambitious expansion program at his hospital.

Benjamin Franklin, at eighty-one, moderated the compromise that led to the adoption of our American Constitution.

I went to see Dr. Normal Vincent Peale. When he was seventy-eight years old, he had four offices that he worked from: one at the church, one at his apartment building, one at Guideposts magazine, and one at the Foundation for Christian Living. He was walking at least four miles every day. I also went that day to see Bishop Fulton Sheen. Here was a man who was still actively preaching God's Word, spending at least an hour a day in time with the Lord, and playing three or four hours of tennis. Bishop Fulton Sheen was eighty-two years old at the time I saw him.

Don't let the mirror lie to you. You are still you. Don't let the mirror steal your dream. Don't let the mirror rob you of your courage to live. Caleb still had his health but he had something much better. He still had his courage to face life. The obstacles were there that he would have had to overcome forty years ago but he was still willing, with courage, to face those obstacles.

It takes courage to live life at all levels. We need to remember that it takes courage to live life as a child. In our childhood days we have to face new things, different things, strange things, hard times. And yet we live through those years. Some children have to live with courage.

It takes courage to be a young person. I come in here on Saturdays often and sit in pews and wonder what it's like to sit where you sit and look up and wonder if God's going to give me a word and how I pray at that time that God will give me the word that you need. I remember sitting one day in the seat of a fifteen-year-old and wondering what it's like to be fifteen, thinking about that, and thinking of all the stresses and temptations and all the pressure that this society places upon our young people as it dumps its garbage in their head and tries to pull them down some path of destruction or lead them in many, many different ways. It takes courage to be a young person.

It takes courage to be a young adult. It's tough to start out nowadays. It's tough to begin a home. It's tough to build a relationship and make a marriage work. It's hard to keep your vows and to keep things going right. It takes courage to be a young adult.

It takes courage to live the middle years. It seems these are the trickiest years for some people. This is when some people really lose it. Just like David in the Old Testament—he was a great young man. He did well in his young years. He was a wonderful old man. He lived splendidly in his old years. But, my, how he messed up in those middle years. It takes courage to live the middle years.

The challenge is to keep courage in your later years, too. Don't let the mirror steal your strength and courage for living. There are changes, physical, more than just what the mirror shows. Sometimes our hearing dims a little bit. I heard about a man who had just gotten a new hearing aid. He was so proud of it. He said, "It's state of the art, cost me twelve hundred dollars. You can hardly tell I'm wearing it." His friend said, "Well, what kind is it?" He said, "Well, it's about 4:30."

Sometimes our vision is not always like it was. A lady the other day was laughing about the fact that she thought she saw a sign for a garage sale. She pulled into the driveway, got out of the car, and looked at the sign and it said: "This house is protected by Rollins Protection Agency."

Sometimes our memory goes. There was a man who said, "I have a hard time remembering who said a quote. I can remember the quote but I can't remember who said it. I don't know if it was Will Rogers or Elizabeth Taylor who said, 'I never met a man I didn't like.' "

It takes courage to live the later years because sometimes we face terrible losses. We have to learn to live alone. We have to deal with loneliness. That takes a great deal of courage. Some people have to learn to love again and establish new relationships. I heard about a man who finally decided it was time for him to move into a retirement village. He was a striking man. The first day there, a lady kept looking at him. She stared at him for six hours. Finally he went to her and said: "Lady, I'm sorry. It really bothers me that you're staring at me."

She replied, "Oh, I didn't realize I was staring. You remind me so much of my third husband."

"How many husbands have you had?" he asked.

She said, "Two." Well, it takes some courage to learn to love and to live again.

It takes courage to walk into eternity. It's a dream God gave me to tell as many people as I possibly can, as well as I possibly can, that the Word of God tells people that you can walk arm-in-arm with Christ all the way through this life and into eternity; that you don't really have to die; that our Lord Christ has made great provision for you.

The book of Genesis, chapter 50, tells about the death of Joseph. It says in verse 26, "So Joseph died at the age of a hundred and ten. And after they embalmed him, he was placed in a coffin in Egypt." And I thought, what a terrible way for a book to end! And then I looked across the page and the next word is "Exodus."

Dr. Frank Pollard is the Pastor Emeritus of the First Baptist Church of Jackson, Mississippi, a church of which he was the senior pastor from 1974–1980 and again from 1986–2001. In the interim he served as pastor of the First Baptist Church of San Antonio and then as president of the Golden Gate Baptist Theological Seminary. He was the preacher of the Baptist Hour radio program for more than twenty years, and of the Baptist Hour television program for more than a decade. *Time* magazine named him one of the seven outstanding Protestant preachers in America. He is now retired, and he and his wife Jane live in Jackson, Mississippi.